TABLE OF CONTENTS

INTRODUCTION
Contributors...1
Author Introduction..2
Coin Roll Hunting..3
Are My Coins Rare?...4
Coin Shows..5

COIN MINTAGES
All Coin Mintages...6-45

MINT MARKS
Mint Mark Placements...47-73
Missing Mint Marks...74

WIDE AM VS CLOSE AM
Wide AM Penny vs Close AM Penny...76

ERROR AND VARIETIES
Errors and Varieties..77-141
RPM's, RPD's, OMM's, MPD's..143-147
Over Date...148
Small Date vs Large Date...149-151
Abbreviations..153
Error Coin Dates...154-182

OTHER
Coin Grading..184-187
Silver Coins..188
Selling Coins...189-190
Coin Terminology..191-194

Social Media: @couchcollectibles | www.couchcollectibles.com

Contributors

I would like the to thank everyone who contributed to this book and anyone who is subscribed to Couch Collectibles on YouTube, Facebook, Instagram and TikTok.

I would also like to thank all of the paid members of Couch Collectibles. You are greatly appreciated and YOU made the first edition and now the second edition of this book possible!

Contributors

Amanda Deines - Subscriber of Couch Collectibles
ae_coins - @ae_coins on Instagram
Bryan Hooper - Bryan Hooper YouTube
Chuck9999 - Chuck9999 eBay store
CoinsTV - www.coinstv.net
Daniel Hickman - Subscriber of Couch Collectibles
Dan T. - Subscriber of Couch Collectibles
Emerson G. - Subscriber of Couch Collectibles
Jeff Chapman - Subscriber of Couch Collectibles
Justin Couch - Couch Collectibles YouTube
Mike G - Subscriber of Couch Collectibles
PCGS (Professional Coin Grading Service) - www.pcgs.com
Rodney S. - Subscriber of Couch Collectibles
Shelia G - Subscriber of Couch Collectibles
Sylvia Jimenez - Sj's Mixed Adventure's YouTube
Tricia Musi - Subscriber of Couch Collectibles

This book is exactly what the title suggest, "A Guide To Coin Hunting". I believe this book will be extremely helpful for new coin collectors as well as some experienced collectors.

We will cover the basics of which coins to look for when your coin roll hunting or going through your pocket change. Not every single mint error or valuable coin is listed in this book however many coins are shown that I believe you will be happy with. We'll look at coin mint marks, coin mintages, mint errors and varieties, along with other desirable coins. This is not a coin price guide. The goal of this book is to provide some basics of coin collecting and help you learn which coins you should be looking for that can be worth worth more than their face value.

If you'd like to know about coin prices, I have a lot of YouTube videos on Couch Collectibles YouTube channel that show you what coins have sold for at previous auctions. For now, I'd say this book is a great start for you coin collectors out there. I hope you are having an awesome day. Let's just hop right into it!

Introduction

@couchcollectibles

"I'VE BEEN COLLECTING COINS FOR OVER 20 YEARS"

AUTHOR: JUSTIN COUCH

I've been fascinated with coins from a very young age. The designs and history of older silver coins were very intriguing to me and that's when my coin collecting journey began.

My grandma Betty also got me into coin collecting as she had a nice collection as well. Now that I've been collecting coins for over 20 years, I'm sharing my experience with other collectors through my YouTube channel, Couch Collectibles along with my other social media accounts.

I really hope you enjoy this book and hope it helps guide you in the right direction to find some rare and valuable coins. Feel free to comment on my YouTube channel or other social media with any coin questions you may have.

Stay Awesome!
Justin Couch

Coin Roll Hunting

Coin roll hunting has been on the rise thanks to social media videos that show viewers it is possible to find silver coins, old coins, mint error coins and other desirable coins from the bank. A box of rolled pennies cost $25, a nickel box cost $100, dimes are $250, quarters and half dollar coin boxes are $500 per box. Listed below are the 6 steps to coin roll hunting that I personally recommend from my experience.

1.) Contact your Bank: The first rule that I always stress, is to be polite to your bank tellers. These are the individuals you will be dealing with frequently if you are coin roll hunting on a regular basis. You can call your bank or go to your bank in person and ask your tellers if they have a box of pennies, nickels, quarters, etc.

2.) Don't Give Up: Some collectors may get discouraged if their bank doesn't have boxes of coins. All you have to do is ask your bank tellers nicely if they can order you a box of half dollars or any other denomination of coins. Usually they will not have a problem with it. If they cannot do that, then try a different branch. If that doesn't work, see if you can get a few rolls of coins instead of a whole box.

3.) Searching Coins: Once you have your box of rolled coins, you can then begin searching for desirable coins. In this book I will list a variety of different coins to look for from the bank. This will include silver coins, low mintage coins, mint error coins and more!

4.) You found something good, now what?: If you think you've found a valuable coin, you can then send that coin to a coin grading company to have it authenticated, or you could sell it as is online. I will cover coin grading and selling coins later in this book. If you want to be 100% certain that you have a coin that is worth getting graded, you can press the blue join button my YouTube channel and become a level 2 member for me to review images of your coins and get my feedback. I will tell you if I believe you should get your coin graded and if I think the coin is a genuine mint error.

5.) Sell your coins: As stated above, I will cover selling coins later in this book but I do suggest that you research what similar coins have sold for in the past. If you search the coin you have on eBay and click on sold listings, you can get an idea of your coins value. Keep in mind the condition or grade will have a tremendous impact on your coins value.

6) Cashing in Coins: After searching through all of your coins, now you have to cash them back in. I would not cash them in at the same bank you got them from. I have a second bank that has a coin counting machine where I cash my coins in for free. As long as I have over $200 in my account, it is completely free! Coinstar is too expensive! Some banks may be different. This will save you a lot of time as you won't have to roll your coins back up into coin rolls.

Are my coins rare?

There are many factors when determining a coin's value. Throughout this book we will look at what can make your coin rare and valuable. Let's look at the list below and dive into what coins to look for in your pocket change or even when you're coin roll hunting from the bank.

1.) Low Mintage Coins: These are coins produced in low quantity in comparison to other years. These are often referred to as "key date coins". For an example the 1909 S V.D.B wheat penny has a low mintage of 484,000. Compare that to the 2016 penny where the mint produced over 4 billion of those no mint mark Lincoln cents.

2.) Coin Mint Marks: Many new collectors get mint marks and values confused. If your penny doesn't have a mint mark, that does not necessarily mean that your coin is valuable. However the 1990 S proof penny with no mint mark can be extremely valuable depending on the condition of the coin. We'll go more in depth on that throughout this book.

3.) Grade / Condition: You can submit your coins to a coin grading company to get a rating in which indicates how much a coin has worn from circulation. The coin grading scale goes from 1-70. Typically the closer your coin is to seventy, the more valuable it can be.

4.) Silver / Gold Coins: Precious metals will always have value in my opinion however some of your silver and gold coins will have more numismatic value than the actual metal value itself. For an example if silver prices are $14.95 per ounce, a silver quarter would have the silver value of roughly $2.70, however the numismatic value of the coin can be much more depending on the date, mint mark, mintage, and condition or grade of the coin.

5.) Grade Population: The grade population is very important when determining a coins value. This will also be based on the market and what collectors are willing pay for a coin.

Justin started coin roll hunting live streams on YouTube in 2017 and was featured on Matty Cardrople's podcast at the Long Beach Expo Coin Show in 2023.

For an example if only one 1990 Lincoln cent graded at a MS-70 exist in the world, the demand for that coin would be high in which would increase the value of the coin. (I'm unsure of the exact population for that specific coin for each grade. I'm only using that as an example.)

Keep in mind, a coins value can fluctuate based on the time in which you sell the coin. The market fluctuates during different periods of time, especially with a change in our economy.

Enough with reading, let's look at some coin images and show you what to look for. I've never been good at reading books so I want to make this read as simple as possible, especially for you new collectors.

We will have coin terms listed towards the end of the book so if you don't quite understand what I am talking about, please refer to the terminology pages.

Let's start off first with coin mintage's then we will look at a list of errors coins to look for.

Coin Shows

What should you know?

Whether your attending a local coin show or large coin show, here are some of my experiences and advice before you attend.

This is the best place in my opinion to get the best deals when purchasing or selling your coins.

In person interactions with real coin dealers give you an opportunity to negotiate a deal without shipping cost, fees, etc. I recently completed my Walking Liberty half dollar coin collection by purchasing my last four coins at a coin show, which was cheaper than it would have been online or even at my local coin shop.

My advice is to be respectful and realistic when communicating with coin dealers. They will be aggravated if you low ball them. Give fair and honest prices of what you want for your coins or what you will pay for their coins.

Blake Alma from CoinHub and Justin Couch from Couch Collectibles meet at the Cincinnati Coin Show.

This leads to developing a relationship. Maybe one dealer has a few coins you would like to purchase. So offer him/her full price for one of the coins and try to bundle the other coins into the deal for a lower overall price.

The last day of a 3-4 day coin show event seems to be the best day for deals. Coin dealers have made their profit for a few days and want to unload their remaining inventory. Don't miss the last day!

If you see me at a coin show, please come and say hi! I'd be happy to speak and conversate with you about coins! I may just give you a free coin roll hunting mat or coin book!

Blake Alma from CoinHub and Justin Couch from Couch Collectibles went up against BlueRidgeSilverhound and Rene from Storage Wars in a coin grading contest at the ANA Coin show in Pittsburg, PA. (we lost but still received these awesome coins) Thanks to Mike from Whatnot!

Coin Mintages

Low Mintage Coins: These are coins produced in low quantity in comparison to other years and are sometimes refereed to as key date coins. For an example the 1909 S V.D.B wheat penny has a low mintage of 484,000. Compare that to the 2016 penny where the mint produced over 4 billion of those no mint mark Lincoln cents.

Indian Head Cent

Image: Justin Couch

Year	Mintage
1859	36,400,000
1860	20,566,000
1861	10,100,000
1862	28,075,000
1863	49,840,000
1864 (Copper)	13,740,000
1864 (Bronze)	39,233,714
1865	35,429,286
1866	9,826,500
1867	9,821,000
1868	10,266,500
1869	6,420,000
1870	5,275,000
1871	3,929,500
1872	4,042,000
1873	11,676,500
1874	14,187,500
1875	13,528,000
1876	7,944,000
1877	**852,500**
1878	5,799,850
1879	16,231,200
1880	38,964,955
1881	39,211,575
1882	38,581,100
1883	45,589,109
1884	23,261,742
1885	11,765,384
1886	17,654,290
1887	45,226,483
1888	37,494,414
1889	48,869,361
1890	57,182,854
1891	47,072,350
1892	37,649,832
1893	46,642,195
1894	16,752,132
1895	38,343,636
1896	39,057,293
1897	50,466,330
1898	49,823,079
1899	53,600,031
1900	66,833,794
1901	79,611,143
1902	87,376,722
1903	85,094,493
1904	61,328,015
1905	80,719,163
1906	96,022,255
1907	108,138,618
1908	32,327,987
1908 S	**1,115,000**
1909	14,370,645
1909 S	**309,000**

The Indian Head one cent coin was designed by James Barton Longacre, the Chief Engraver at the Philadelphia Mint.

- **Composition of Coin:** (1859–1864) 88% copper, 12% nickel, (1864–1909) 95% copper, 5% tin and zinc.
- **Years of minting:** 1858 (patterns only), 1859–1909 (regular issues)
- **Mint marks:** "S" will be located below the wreath on the reverse. Philadelphia Mint specimens were struck without a mint mark.
- **Diameter:** 19.05 mm (0.750 in)
- **Edge:** Plain
- **Weight:** (1859–1864) 4.67 grams, (1864–1909) 3.11 grams

Key Dates
1864 (L on ribbon)
1877
1908 S
1909 S

Coin Mintages
Lincoln Wheat Cent Mintage

1909 72,702,618
1909 VDB 27,995,000
1909 S   1,825,000
1909 S VDB 484,000
1910   146,801,218
1910 S   6,045,000
1911   101,177,787
1911 D 12,672,000
1911 S   4,026,000
1912   68,153,060
1912 D 10,411,000
1912 S   4,431,000
1913   76,532,352
1913 D 15,804,000
1913 S   6,101,000
1914   75,238,432
1914 D 1,193,000
1914 S   4,137,000
1915   29,092,120
1915 D 22,050,000
1915 S   4,833,000
1916   131,833,677
1916 D 35,956,000
1916 S 22,510,000
1917   196,429,785
1917 D 55,120,000
1917 S 32,620,000
1918   288,104,634
1918 D 47,830,000
1918 S 34,680,000
1919   392,021,000
1919 D 57,154,000
1919 S 139,760,000
1920   310,165,000
1920 D 49,280,000
1920 S 46,220,000
1921   39,157,000
1921 S 15,274,000
1922 D 7,160,000
1923   74,723,000
1923 S   8,700,000
1924   75,178,000
1924 D   2,520,000
1924 S 11,696,000

The Lincoln Wheat Penny was designed by Victor David Brenner. You will notice his V.D.B initials on the reverse of the 1909 and 1909 S mint mark wheat cents at the bottom. His initials are now on the obverse of the coin.

Bronze Lincoln Cents
Dates: (1909-1942), (1947-1962), 2009
Composition: 95% copper, 5% tin and zinc
Weight: 3.11 grams
Diameter: 19 mm

Zinc Coated Steel Lincoln Cents
Date: 1943
Composition: Steel coated with Zinc
Weight: 2.70 grams
Diameter: 19 mm

Copper Lincoln Cent
Dates: (1944-1946), (1962-1982)
Composition: 95% copper, 5% zinc
Weight: 3.11 grams
Diameter: 19 mm

1925   139,949,000
1925 D 22,580,000
1925 S 26,380,000
1926   157,088,000
1926 D 28,020,000
1926 S   4,550,000
1927   144,440,000
1927 D 27,170,000
1927 S 14,276,000
1928   134,116,000
1928 D 31,170,000
1928 S 17,266,000
1929   185,262,000
1929 D 41,730,000
1929 S 50,148,000

1930   157,415,000
1930 D 40,100,000
1930 S 24,286,000
1931   19,396,000
1931 D   4,480,000
1931 S   866,000
1932   9,062,000
1932 D 10,500,000
1933   14,360,000
1933 D   6,200,000
1934   219,080,000
1934 D 28,446,000
1935   245,388,000
1935 D 47,000,000
1935 S 38,702,000
1936   309,632,000
1936 D 40,620,000
1936 S 29,130,000
1937   309,170,000
1937 D 50,430,000
1937 S 34,500,000
1938   156,682,000
1938 D 20,010,000

Coin Mintages

Lincoln Wheat Cent Mintage

1938 S	15,180,000	1953 D	700,515,000	
1939	316,466,000	1953 S	181,835,000	
1939 D	15,160,000	1954	71,640,050	
1939 S	52,070,000	1954 D	251,552,500	
1940	586,810,000	1954 S	96,190,000	
1940 D	81,390,000	1955	330,958,200	
1940 S	112,940,000	1955 D	563,257,500	
1941	887,018,000	1955 S	44,610,000	
1941 D	128,700,000	1956	420,745,000	
1941 S	92,360,000	1956 D	1,098,201,100	
1942	657,796,000	1957	282,540,000	
1942 D	206,698,000	1957 D	1,051,342,000	
1942 S	85,590,000	1958	252,525,000	
1943	684,628,670	1958 D	800,953,300	
1943 D	217,660,000			
1943 S	191,550,000			
1944	1,435,400,000			
1944 D	430,578,000			
1944 S	282,760,000			
1945	1,040,515,000			
1945 D	266,268,000			
1945 S	181,770,000			
1946	991,655,000			
1946 D	315,690,000			
1946 S	198,100,000			
1947	190,555,000			
1947 D	194,750,000			
1947 S	99,000,000			
1948	317,570,000			
1948 D	172,637,500			
1948 S	81,735,000			
1949	217,775,000			
1949 D	153,132,500			
1949 S	64,290,000			
1950	272,635,000			
1950 D	334,950,000			
1950 S	118,505,000			
1951	284,576,000			
1951 D	625,355,000			
1951 S	136,010,000			
1952	186,775,000			
1952 D	746,130,000			
1952 S	137,800,004			
1953	256,755,000			

Key Dates
1909 S
1909 S V.D.B
1914 D
1922 Plain (No D Strong Reverse)
1931 S

1943 Lincoln cents were struck using steel due to wartime shortages of copper. There are some authentic examples of the 1944 steel cent that are extremely rare and valuable. Don't forget about the holy grail, 1943 copper cent that sells for tens of thousands of dollars. Below you will see the weight for Lincoln cents. Another coin you want to look for is the 1983 Lincoln cent struck on a copper planchet that weights 3.1 grams.

Lincoln Cent 1982-Present

- **Value:** 0.01 U.S. Dollars
- **Weight:** (1982-present) 2.5 grams
- **Diameter:** 19.05 mm (0.75 in)
- **Thickness:** 1.52 mm (0.0598 in)
- **Edge:** Plain
- **Composition:** (1982–present) copper-plated zinc, 97.5% Zinc, 2.5% Copper

800,000+ SUBSCRIBERS!

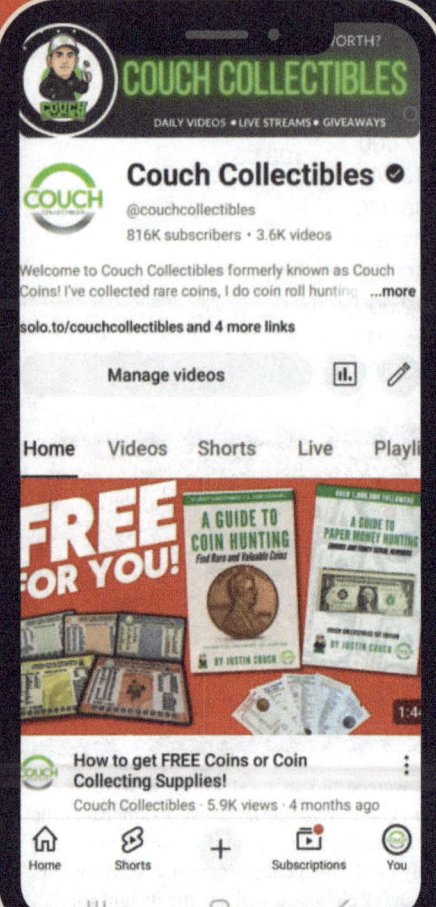

COIN PRICES & FREE SILVER COIN GIVEAWAYS!

BECOME A LEVEL 2 MEMBER FOR ME TO REVIEW YOUR COIN IMAGES!

Press the blue Join button on my YouTube channel

SUBSCRIBE TO COUCH COLLECTIBLES IT'S FREE!

SCAN ME

Coin Mintages

Two Cent Piece Mintage

1864 19,822,500
1865 13,640,000
1866 3,177,000
1867 2,938,750
1868 2,803,750
1869 1,546,500
1870 861,250
1871 721,250
1872 65,000
1873 Proof Only

The two cent piece was designed by James B. Longacre and minted from 1864-1873.

Two Cent Piece 1864-1873
- **Value:** 0.02 U.S. Dollars
- **Weight:** 6.22 grams
- **Diameter:** 23.00 mm
- **Edge:** Plain
- **Composition:** 95 % copper, 5 % tin and zinc
- **Mint Marks:** None (all struck at the Philadelphia Mint)

Coin Mintages

Silver Three Cent Piece Mintage

1851 5,447,400
1851-O 720,000
1852 18,663,500
1853 11,400,000
1854 671,000
1855 139,000
1856 1,458,000
1857 1,042,000
1858 1,603,700
1859 364,200
1860 286,000
1861 497,000
1862 343,000
1863 21,000
1864 12,000
1865 8,000
1866 22,000
1867 4,000
1868 3,500
1869 4,500
1870 3,000
1871 3,400
1872 1,000
1873 Proof Only

The silver three cent piece was designed by the Mint's chief engraver, James B. Longacre and minted from 1851-1873.

- **Value:** 0.03 U.S. Dollars
- **Weight:** 1851–1853, .80 g. Later pieces, .75 g
- **Diameter:** 14 mm
- **Edge:** Plain
- **Composition:** 1851–1853, .0193 troy oz. Later issues, .0217 troy oz
- **Mint Marks:** O (1851 only). To the right of the Roman numeral on the reverse. Philadelphia Mint specimens struck without mint mark.

Florence man becomes coin-collecting YouTube sensation

11

Coin Mintages
Nickel Three Cent Piece Mintage

1865 11,382,000
1866 4,801,000
1867 3,915,000
1868 3,252,000
1869 1,604,000
1870 1,335,000
1871 604,000
1872 862,000
1873, Close 3 390,000
1873, Open 3 783,000
1874 790,000
1875 228,000
1876 162,000
1877 Proof Only
1878 Proof Only
1879 38,000
1880 21,000
1881 1,077,000
1882 22,200
1883 4,000
1884 1,700
1885 1,000
1886 Proof Only
1887 5,001
1888 36,501
1889 18,125

The nickel three cent piece was designed by the Mint's chief engraver, James B. Longacre and minted from 1865-1889.

- **Value:** 0.03 U.S. Dollars
- **Weight:** 1.94g
- **Diameter:** 17.9 mm
- **Edge:** Plain
- **Composition:** 75% copper, 25% nickel
- **Mint Marks:** None, all were struck at Philadelphia Mint without a mint mark.

Coin Mintages

Liberty Head V Nickel: These five cent coins are often referred to as "V Nickels" as a large "V" is represented on the reverse of the coin. The obverse of the coin features the "Goddess of Liberty".

Liberty Head V Nickel Mintage

1883 with CENTS 16,026,200
1883 without CENTS 5,474,300
1884 11,270,000
1885 1,473,300
1886 3,326,000
1887 15,260,692
1888 10,715,901
1889 15,878,025
1890 16,256,532
1891 16,832,000
1892 11,696,897
1893 13,368,000
1894 5,410,500
1895 9,977,822
1896 8,841,048
1897 20,426,797
1898 12,530,292
1899 26,027,000
1900 27,253,733
1901 26,478,228
1902 31,487,581
1903 28,004,930
1904 21,403,167
1905 29,825,124
1906 38,612,000
1907 39,213,325
1908 22,684,557
1909 11,585,763
1910 30,166,948
1911 39,557,639
1912 26,234,569
1912-D 8,474,000
1912-S 238,000
1913 5 Known

Image: Justin Couch

The Indian Head one cent coin was designed by Mint Chief Engraver Charles Barber.

- **Composition of Coin:** 75% copper, 25% nickel.
- **Years of minting:** 1883-1913
- **Mint marks:** No Mint Mark, D Mint Mark and S Mint Marks.
- **Diameter:** 21.21 mm (0.8350 in)
- **Edge:** Plain
- **Weight:** 5.0 g (0.1615 troy oz)

Coin Mintages
Buffalo Nickel Mintage

1913 Variety 1 30,993,520
1913 D Variety 1 5,337,000
1913 S Variety 1 2,105,000
1913 Variety 2 29,858,700
1913 D Variety 2 4,156,000
1913 S Variety 2 1,290,000
1914 20,665,738
1914 D 3,912,000
1914 S 3,470,000
1915 20,987,270
1915 D 7,569,000
1915 S 1,505,000
1916 63,498,066
1916 D 13,333,000
1916 S 11,860,000
1917 51,424,019
1917 D 9,910,000
1917 S 4,193,000
1918 32,086,314
1918 D 8,362,000
1918 S 4,882,000
1919 60,868,000
1919 D 8,006,000
1919 S 7,521,000
1920 63,093,000
1920 D 9,418,000
1920 S 9,689,000
1921 10,663,000
1921 S 1,557,000
1923 35,715,000
1923 S 6,142,000
1924 21,620,000
1924 D 5,258,000
1924 S 1,437,000
1925 35,565,100
1925 D 4,450,000
1925 S 6,256,000
1926 44,693,000
1926 D 5,638,000
1926 S 970,000
1927 37,981,000
1927 D 5,730,000
1927 S 3,430,000

1928 23,411,000
1928 D 6,436,000
1928 S 6,936,000
1929 36,446,000
1929 D 8,370,000
1929 S 7,754,000
1930 22,849,000
1930 S 5,435,000
1931 S 1,200,000
1934 20,213,003
1934 D 7,480,000
1935 58,264,000
1935 D 12,092,000
1935 S 10,300,000
1936 119,001,420
1936 D 24,814,000
1936 S 14,930,000
1937 79,485,769
1937 D 17,826,000
1937 S 5,635,000
1938 D 7,020,000

The Buffalo Nickel or sometimes referred to as the Indian Head Nickel was designed by sculptor James Earle Fraser.

- **Years of minting:** 1913–1938
- **Mint marks:** D, S. under "FIVE CENTS" on the reverse at the bottom of the coin. Philadelphia Mint nickels did not have a mint mark.
- **Value:** 5 cents (.05 US dollars)
- **Composition:** 75% copper, 25% nickel
- **Diameter:** 21 mm (0.8350 in)
- **Edge:** Plain
- **Weight:** 5.0 grams

Key Dates
1913 S Type 2
1915 S
1918/7 D
1921 S
1924 S
1926 S
1937 D 3-Legged

Coin Mintages
Jefferson Nickel Mintage

Year	Mintage
1938	19,496,000
1938 D	5,376,000
1938 S	4,105,000
1939	120,615,000
1939 D	**3,514,000**
1939 S	6,630,000
1940	176,485,000
1940 D	43,540,000
1940 S	39,690,000
1941	203,265,000
1941 D	53,432,000
1941 S	43,445,000
1942	49,789,000
1942 D	13,938,000
1942 P Silver	57,873,000
1942 S Silver	32,900,000
1943 P Silver	271,165,000
1943 D Silver	15,294,000
1943 S Silver	104,060,000
1944 P Silver	119,150,000
1944 D Silver	32,309,000
1944 S Silver	21,640,000
1945 P Silver	119,408,100
1945 D Silver	37,158,000
1945 S Silver	58,939,000
1946	161,116,000

The Jefferson nickel featuring Thomas Jefferson was designed by Felix Schlag. The obverse design used in 2005 was designed by Joe Fitzgerald. Since 2006, the design used was created by Jamie Franki.

- **Years of minting:** 1938 – present
- **Value:** 5 cents (0.05 US dollars)
- **Edge:** Plain
- **Weight:** 5.0 grams
- **Composition:** 75% copper, 25% nickel "Wartime Nickels" (mid-1942 to 1945): 56% copper, 35% silver, 9% manganese

Year	Mintage	Year	Mintage
1946 D	45,292,200	1952 S	20,572,000
1946 S	13,560,000	1953	46,644,000
1947	95,000,000	1953 D	59,878,600
1947 D	37,822,000	1953 S	19,210,900
1947 S	24,720,000	1954	47,684,050
1948	89,348,000	1954 D	117,183,060
1948 D	44,734,000	1954 S	29,384,000
1948 S	11,300,000	1955	7,888,000
1949	60,652,000	1955 D	74,464,100
1949 D	36,498,000	1956	35,216,000
1949 S	9,716,000	1956 D	67,222,940
1950	9,796,000	1957	38,408,000
1950 D	**2,630,030**	1957 D	136,828,900
1951	28,552,000	1958	17,088,000
1951 D	20,460,000	1958 D	168,249,120
1951 S	7,776,000	1959	27,248,000
1952	63,988,000	1959 D	160,738,240
1952 D	30,638,000		

Key Dates
1939 D
1950 D

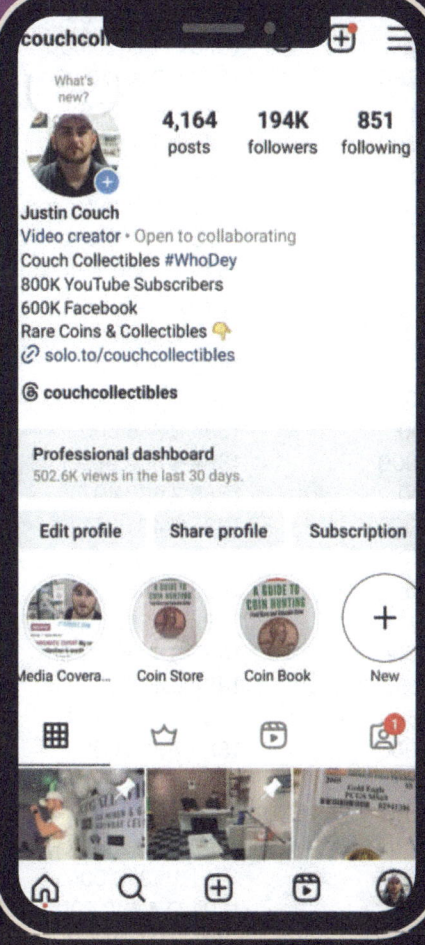

100,000+ FOLLOWERS!

DAILY
COIN VIDEOS AND IMAGES ON INSTAGRAM!

@COUCHCOLLECTIBLES

SCAN ME

FOLLOW COUCH COLLECTIBLES IT'S FREE!

Liberty Seated Dime Mintage

Stars on Obverse
1838 1,992,500
1839 1,053,115
1839-O 1,323,000
1840 981,500
1840-O 1,175,000
1840 377,500
1841 1,622,500
1841-O 2,007,500
1842 1,887,500
1842-O 2,020,000
1843 1,370,000
1843-O 150,000
1844 72,500
1845 1,755,000
1845-O 230,000
1846 31,300
1847 245,000
1848 451,500
1849 839,000
1849-O 300,000
1850 1,931,500
1850-O 510,000
1851 1,026,500
1851-O 400,000
1852 1,535,500
1852-O 430,000
1853 No arrows 95,000

Arrows at Date
1853 With Arrows 12,078,010
1853-O 1,100,000
1854 4,470,000
1854-O 1,770,000
1855 2,075,000

Stars on Obverse
1856 5,780,000
1856-O 1,180,000
1856-S 70,000
1857 5,580,000
1857-O 1,540,000
1858 1,540,000
1858-O 290,000
1858-S 60,000
1859 430,000
1859-O 480,000
1859-S 60,000   1860-S 140,000

Legend on Obverse
1860 606,000
1860-O 40,000
1861 1,883,000
1861-S 172,500
1862 847,000
1862-S 180,750
1863 14,000
1863-S 157,500
1864 11,000
1864-S 230,000
1865 10,000
1865-S 175,000
1866 8,000
1866-S 135,000
1867 6,000
1867-S 140,000
1868 464,000
1868-S 260,000
1869 256,000
1869-S 450,000
1870 470,500
1870-S 50,000
1871 906,750
1871-S 320,000
1871-CC 20,100
1872 2,395,500
1872-S 190,000
1872-CC 35,480
1873 No Arrows 1,568,000
1873-CC No Arrows Unique

Arrows at Date
1873 2,377,700
1873-S 455,000
1873-CC 18,791
1874 2,939,300
1874-S 240,000
1874-CC 10,817

Legend on Obverse
1875 10,350,000
1875-S 9,070,000
1875-CC 4,645,000
1876 11,460,000
1876-S 10,420,000
1876-CC 8,270,000
1877 7,310,000
1877-S 2,340,000
1877-CC 7,700,000
1878 1,677,200
1878-CC 200,000
1879 14,000
1880 36,000
1881 24,000
1882 3,910,000
1883 7,674,673
1884 3,365,505
1884-S 564,969
1885 2,532,497
1885-S 43,690
1886 6,376,684
1886-S 206,524
1887 11,283,229
1887-S 4,454,450
1888 5,495,655
1888-S 1,720,000
1889 7,380,000
1889-S 972,678
1890 9,910,951
1890-S 1,423,076
1891 15,310,000
1891-O 4,540,000
1891-S 3,196,116

The Liberty Seated dime design was created by Christian Gobrecht.

- **Years of minting:** 1837-1891
- **Value:** 10 cents (0.10 US dollars)
- **Composition:** .900 silver .100 copper
- **Edge:** reeded
- **Weight:** 2.67 grams to 2.49 grams in 1853, 2.50 grams in 1873

Coin Mintages

Barber Dime Mintage

1892 12,120,000
1892-O 3,841,700
1892-S 990,710
1893 3,340,000
1893-O 1,760,000
1893-S 2,491,401
1894 1,330,000
1894-O 720,000
1895 690,000
1895-O 440,000
1895-S 1,120,000
1896 2,000,000
1896-O 610,000
1896-S 575,056
1897 10,868,533
1897-O 666,000
1897-S 1,342,844
1898 16,320,000
1898-O 2,130,000
1898-S 1,702,507
1899 19,850,000
1899-O 2,650,000
1899-S 1,867,493
1900 17,600,000
1900-O 2,010,000
1900-S 5,168,270
1901 18,859,665
1901-O 5,620,000
1901-S 593,022
1902 21,380,000
1902-O 4,500,000
1902-S 2,070,000
1903 19,500,000
1903-O 8,180,000
1903-S 613,300
1904 14,600,357
1904-S 800,000

The silver Barber dime design was created by Charles E. Barber.

- **Years of minting:** 1892-1916
- **Silver:** 0.07234 troy oz
- **Value:** 10 cents (0.10 US dollars)
- **Composition:** .900 silver .100 copper
- **Edge:** reeded
- **Weight:** 2.500 grams

1905 14,551,623
1905-O 3,400,000
1905-S 6,855,199
1906 19,957,731
1906-D 4,060,000
1906-O 2,610,000
1906-S 3,136,640
1907 22,220,000
1907-D 4,080,000

Coin Mintages

Mercury Dime Mintage

Year	Mintage
1916	22,180,080
1916 D	**264,000**
1916 S	10,450,000
1917	55,230,000
1917 D	9,402,000
1917 S	27,330,000
1918	26,680,000
1918 D	22,674,800
1918 S	19,300,000
1919	35,740,000
1919 D	9,939,000
1919 S	8,850,000
1920	59,030,000
1920 D	19,171,000
1920 S	13,820,000
1921	**1,230,000**
1921 D	**1,080,000**
1923	50,130,000
1923 S	6,440,000
1924	24,010,000
1924 D	6,810,000
1924 S	7,120,000
1925	25,610,000
1925 D	5,117,000
1925 S	5,850,000
1926	32,160,000
1926 D	6,828,000
1926 S	**1,520,000**
1927	28,080,000
1927 D	4,812,000
1927 S	4,770,000
1928	19,480,000
1928 D	4,161,000
1928 S	7,400,000
1929	25,970,000
1929 D	5,034,000
1929 S	4,730,000
1930	6,770,000
1930 S	**1,843,000**
1931	3,150,000
1931 D	**1,260,000**
1931 S	**1,800,000**
1934	24,080,000
1934 D	6,772,000
1935	58,830,000
1935 D	10,477,000
1935 S	15,840,000
1936	87,500,000
1936 D	16,132,000
1936 S	9,210,000
1937	56,860,000
1937 D	14,146,000
1937 S	9,740,000
1938	22,190,000
1938 D	5,537,000
1938 S	8,090,000
1939	67,740,000
1939 D	24,394,000
1939 S	10,540,000
1940	65,350,000
1940 D	21,198,000
1940 S	21,560,000
1941	175,090,000
1941 D	45,634,000
1941 S	43,090,000
1942	205,410,000
1942 D	60,740,000
1942 S	49,300,000
1943	191,710,000
1943 D	71,949,000
1943 S	60,400,000
1944	231,410,000
1944 D	62,224,000
1944 S	49,490,000
1945	159,130,000
1945 D	40,245,000
1945 S	41,290,000

The Mercury dime design was created by Adolph Weinman.

- **Years of minting:** 1916–1945 for commerce, 2016 as a gold commemorative
- **Silver:** 0.07234 troy oz, 90% Silver, Gold: (2016 only) 0.10000 troy oz
- **Value:** 10 cents (0.10 US dollars)
- **Composition:** .900 silver .100 copper, 2016: .9999 gold
- **Edge:** 118 reeds
- **Weight:** 2.500 grams, except 2016 gold issue: 3.110 grams

Key Dates
1916 D
1921
1921 D
1942/1
1942/1 D

Coin Mintages

Roosevelt Dime Mintage

Year	Mintage
1946	255,250,000
1946 D	61,043,500
1946 S	27,900,000
1947	121,520,000
1947 D	46,835,000
1947 S	34,840,000
1948	74,950,000
1948 D	52,841,000
1948 S	35,520,000
1949	30,940,000
1949 D	26,034,000
1949 S	**13,510,000**
1950	50,130,114
1950 D	46,803,000
1950 S	20,440,000
1951	103,880,102
1951 D	56,529,000
1951 S	31,630,000
1952	99,040,093
1952 D	122,100,000
1952 S	44,419,500
1953	53,490,120
1953 D	136,433,000
1953 S	39,180,000
1954	114,010,203
1954 D	106,397,000
1954 S	22,860,000
1955	**12,450,181**
1955 D	**13,959,000**
1955 S	**18,510,000**
1956	108,640,000
1956 D	108,015,100
1957	160,160,000
1957 D	113,354,330
1958	31,910,000
1958 D	136,564,600
1959	85,780,000
1959 D	164,919,790
1960	70,390,000
1960 D	200,160,400
1961	93,730,000
1961 D	209,146,550
1962	72,450,000
1962 D	334,948,380
1963	123,650,000
1963 D	421,476,530
1964	929,360,000
1964 D	1,357,517,180

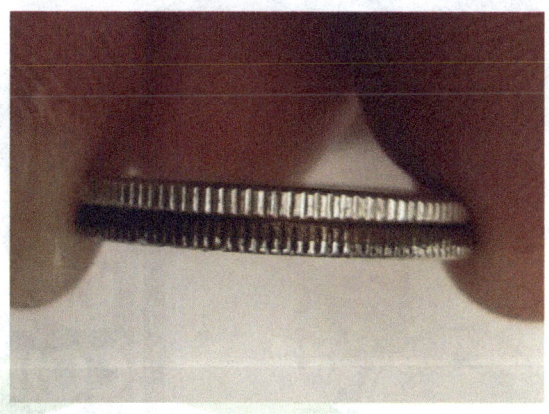

The above images is displaying the different edges of a silver Roosevelt dime versus a clad dime. The dime on top is 90% silver.

The Roosevelt dime was designed by Chief Engraver John R. Sinnock.

- **Years of minting:** 1946 - Present
- **Silver:** 0.07234 troy oz, 90% Silver (1946-1964)
- **Value:** 10 cents (0.10 US dollars)
- **Edge:** reeded
- **Diameter:** 17.91 mm (0.705 in)
- **Weight:** 2.268 grams (1965 - Present), 2.5 grams (Pre-1964)

Key Dates
1949 S
1955
1955 D
1955 S

600,000+ FOLLOWERS!

DAILY
COIN VIDEOS AND LIVE STREAMS ON FACEBOOK!

@COUCHCOLLECTIBLES

SCAN ME

FOLLOW COUCH COLLECTIBLES IT'S FREE!

21

Coin Mintages
Liberty Seated Quarter Mintage

1838 No Drapery 466,000
1839 No Drapery 491,146
1840 No Drapery 188,127
1840-O No Drapery 382,200
1840-O Drapery 43,000
1841 120,000
1841-O 452,000
1842 88,000
1842-O 769,000
1843 645,600
1843-O 968,000
1844 421,200
1844-O 740,000
1845 922,000
1846 510,000
1847 734,000
1847-O 368,000
1848 146,000
1849 340,000
1850-O 412,000
1850 190,800
1851 160,000
1851-O 88,000
1852 177,060
1852-O 96,000
1853 44,200
1853 Arrows and Rays 15,210,020
1853-O Arrows and Rays 1,332,000
1854 Arrows 12,380,000
1854-O Arrows 1,484,000
1855 Arrows 2,857,000
1855-O Arrows 176,000
1855-S Arrows 396,400
1856 7,264,000
1856-O 968,000
1856-S 286,000
1857 9,644,000
1857-O 1,180,000
1857-S 82,000
1858 7,368,000
1858 Proof 300
1858-O 520,000
1858-S 121,000

The Liberty Seated Quarter was designed by Robert Ball Hughes and Christian Gobrecht.

- **Years of minting:** 1838-1891
- **Composition:** 90% Silver, 10% Copper
- **Value:** 25 cents (0.25 US dollars)
- **Diameter:** 24.3 mm
- **Edge:** reeded
- **Weight:** 6.25 g

1859 1,343,200
1859 Proof 800
1859-O 260,000
1859-S 80,000
1860 804,400
1860 Proof 1,000
1860-O 388,000
1860-S 56,000
1861 4,853,600
1861 Proof 1,000
1861-S 96,000
1862 932,000
1862 Proof 550
1862-S 67,000
1863 191,600
1863 Proof 460
1864 93,600
1864 Proof 470
1864-S 20,000
1865 58,800
1965 Proof 500
1865-S 41,000

1866 16,800
1866 Proof 725
1866-S 28,000
1867 20,000
1867 Proof 625
1867-S 48,000
1868 29,400
1868 Proof 600
1868-S 96,000
1869 16,000
1869 Proof 600
1869-S 76,000
1870 86,400
1870 Proof 1,000
1870-CC 8,340
1871 118,200
1871 Proof 960
1871-S 30,900
1871-CC 10,890
1872 182,000
1872 Proof 950

Coin Mintages

Liberty Seated Quarter Mintage

1872-S 83,000
1872-CC 22,850
1873 Close 3 40,000
1873 Proof Close 3 600
1873 Open 3 172,000
1873-CC 4,000
1873-CC Proof 6 Known
1873 Arrows 1,271,160
1873 Proof Arrows 500
1873-S Arrows 156,000
1873-CC Arrows 12,462
1874 Arrows 471,200
1874 Proof Arrows 700
1874-S Arrows 392,000
1875 4,292,800
1875 Proof 700
1875-S 680,000
1875-CC 140,000
1876 17,816,000
1876 Proof 1,150
1876-S 8,596,000
1876-CC 4,944,000
1877 10,911,200
1877 Proof 510
1877-S 8,996,000
1877-CC 4,192,000
1878 2,260,000
1878 Proof 800
1878-S 140,000
1878-CC 996,000
1879 13,600
1879 Proof 1,100
1880 13,600
1880 Proof 1,355
1881 12,000
1881 Proof 975
1882 15,200
1882 Proof 1,100
1883 14,400
1883 Proof 1,039

1884 8,000
1884 Proof 875
1885 13,600
1885 Proof 930
1886 5,000
1886 Proof 886
1887 10,000
1887 Proof 710
1888 10,001
1888 Proof 832
1888-S 1,216,000
1889 12,000
1889 Proof 711
1890 80,000
1890 Proof 590
1891 3,920,000
1891 Proof 600
1891-O 68,000
1891-S 2,216,000

23

Coin Mintages

Barber Quarter Mintage

1892 8,236,000	1903 9,669,309
1892 Proof 1,245	1903 Proof 755
1892-O 2,640,000	1903-O 3,500,000
1892-S 964,079	1903-S 1,036,000
1893 5,444,023	1904 9,588,143
1893 Proof 792	1904 Proof 670
1893-O 3,396,000	1904-O 2,456,000
1893-S 1,454,535	1905 4,967,523
1894 3,432,000	1905 Proof 727
1894 Proof 972	1905-O 1,230,000
1894-O 2,852,000	1905-S 1,884,000
1894-S 2,648,821	1906 3,655,760
1895 4,440,000	1906 Proof 675
1895 Proof 880	1906-D 3,280,000
1895-O 2,816,000	1906-O 2,056,000
1895-S 1,764,681	1907 7,192,000
1896 3,874,000	1907 Proof 575
1896 Proof 762	1907-D 2,484,000
1896-O 1,484,000	1907-O 4,560,000
1896-S 188,039	1907-S 1,360,000
1897 8,140,000	1908 4,232,000
1897 Proof 731	1908 Proof 545
1897-O 1,414,800	1908-D 5,788,000
1897-S 542,229	1908-O 6,244,000
1898 11,100,000	1908-S 784,000
1898 Proof 735	1909 9,268,000
1898-O 1,868,000	1909 Proof 650
1898-S 1,020,592	1909-D 5,114,000
1899 12,624,000	1909-O 712,000
1899 Proof 846	1909-S 1,348,000
1899-O 2,644,000	1910 2,244,000
1899-S 708,000	1910 Proof 551
1900 10,016,000	1910-D 1,500,000
1900 Proof 912	1911 3,720,000
1900-O 3,416,000	1911 Proof 543
1900-S 1,858,585	1911-D 933,600	1914 6,244,230
1901 8,892,000	1911-S 988,000	1914 Proof 380
1901 Proof 813	1912 4,400,000	1914-D 3,046,000
1901-O 1,612,000	1912 Proof 700	1914-S 264,000
1901-S 72,664	1912-S 708,000	1915 3,480,000
1902 12,196,967	1913 484,000	1915 Proof 450
1902 Proof 777	1913 Proof 613	1915-D 3,694,000
1902-O 4,748,000	1913-D 1,450,800	1915-S 704,000
1902-S 1,524,612	1913-S 40,000	1916 1,788,000

The Barber Quarter was designed by by sculptor Charles E. Barber.

- **Years of minting:** 1891-1916
- **Composition:** 90% Silver, 10% Copper
- **Value:** 25 cents (0.25 US dollars)
- **Diameter:** 24.3 mm
- **Edge:** reeded
- **Weight:** 6.25 g

24

Coin Mintages

Standing Liberty Quarter Mintage

1916 52,000
1917 Variety 1 8,740,000
1917-D Variety 1 1,509,200
1917-S Variety 1 1,952,000
1917 Variety 2 13,880,000
1917-D Variety 2 6,224,400
1917-S Variety 2 5,552,000
1918 14,240,000
1918-D 7,380,800
1918-S 11,072,000
1919 11,324,000
1919-D 1,944,000
1919-S 1,836,000
1920 27,860,000
1920-D 3,586,400
1920-S 6,380,000
1921 1,916,000
1923 9,716,000
1923-S 1,360,000
1924 10,920,000
1924-D 3,112,000
1924-S 2,860,000
1925 12,280,000
1926 11,316,000
1926-D 1,716,000
1926-S 2,700,000
1927 11,912,000
1927-D 976,000
1927-S 396,000
1928 6,336,000
1928-D 1,627,600
1928-S 2,644,000
1929 11,140,000
1929-D 1,358,000
1929-S 1,764,000
1930 5,632,000
1930-S 1,556,000

The Standing Liberty Quarter was designed by by sculptor Hermon MacNeil.

- **Years of minting:** 1916-1930
- **Composition:** 90% Silver, 10% Copper
- **Value:** 25 cents (0.25 US dollars)
- **Diameter:** 24.3 mm
- **Edge:** reeded
- **Weight:** 6.25 g

Coin Mintages

Washington Quarter Mintage

1932	5,404,000	1948	35,196,000
1932 D	**436,800**	1948 D	16,766,800
1932 S	**408,000**	1948 S	15,960,000
1934	31,912,052	1949	9,312,000
1934 D	3,527,200	1949 D	10,068,400
1935	32,484,000	1950	24,920,126
1935 D	5,780,000	1950 D	21,075,600
1935 S	5,660,000	1950 S	10,284,004
1936	41,300,000	1951	43,448,102
1936 D	5,374,000	1951 D	35,354,800
1936 S	3,828,000	1951 S	9,048,000
1937	19,696,000	1952	38,780,093
1937 D	7,189,600	1952 D	49,795,200
1937 S	**1,652,000**	1952 S	13,707,800
1938	9,472,000	1953	18,536,120
1938 S	2,832,000	1953 D	56,112,400
1939	33,540,000	1953 S	14,016,000
1939 D	7,092,000	1954	54,412,203
1939 S	2,628,000	1954 D	42,305,500
1940	35,704,000	1954 S	11,834,722
1940 D	2,797,600	1955	18,180,181
1940 S	8,244,000	1955 D	3,182,400
1941	79,032,000	1956	44,144,000
1941 D	16,714,800	1956 D	32,334,500
1941 S	16,080,000	1957	46,532,000
1942	102,096,000	1957 D	77,924,160
1942 D	17,487,200	1958	6,360,000
1942 S	19,384,000	1958 D	78,124,900
1943	99,700,000	1959	24,384,000
1943 D	16,095,600	1959 D	62,054,232
1943 S	21,700,000	1960	29,164,000
1944	104,956,000	1960 D	63,000,324
1944 D	14,600,800	1961	37,036,000
1944 S	12,560,000	1961 D	83,656,928
1945	74,372,000	1962	36,156,000
1945 D	12,341,600	1962 D	127,554,756
1945 S	17,004,001	1963	74,316,000
1946	53,436,000	1963 D	135,288,184
1946 D	9,072,800	1964	560,390,585
1946 S	4,204,000	1964 D	704,135,528
1947	22,556,000		
1947 D	15,388,000		
1947 S	5,532,000		

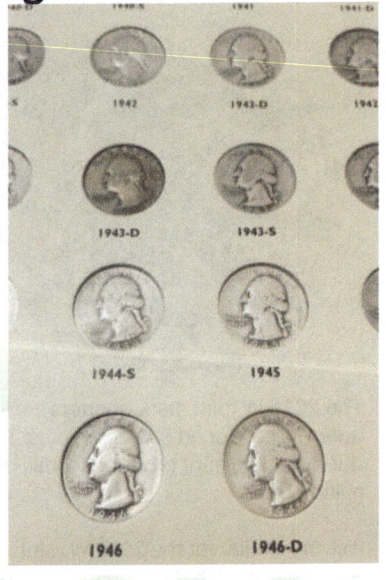

The Washington Quarter was designed by by sculptor John Flanagan.

- **Years of minting:** 1932–present
- **Composition:** (1932-1964) 90% Silver
- **Value:** 25 cents (0.25 US dollars)
- **Diameter:** 24.3 mm
- **Edge:** reeded
- **Weight:** 5.670 grams (1965-Present), 6.25 grams (Pre-1964)

Key Dates
1932 D
1932 S
1937 S

Coin Mintages
Low Mintage Modern Quarters

The 2019 W mint mark quarters are low mintage coins in comparison to other quarters produced in recent years. There are five different reverse designs for these quarters. The mint produced 2 million W mint mark quarters for each design, 10 million total.

It's very similar for the 2020 W mint mark quarters. They will produce 2 million for each design with the W mint mark. The difference for 2020 quarters is that they will also have a V75 privy mark on the obverse of the coin to celebrate the 75th anniversary of the end of the American combat involvement in World War II. You will see that privy mark in the images below. Be on the look out for these in coin rolls from the bank as they are selling very well on eBay. *Images: Justin Couch*

Coin Mintages
Liberty Seated Half Dollar Mintage

No Motto Above Eagle

1839 1,972,400
1840 1,435,008
1840-O 855,100
1841 310,000
1841-O 401,000
1842 2,012,764
1842-O Medium Date 957,000
1843 3,844,000
1843-O 2,268,000
1844 1,766,000
1844-O 2,005,000
1845 589,000
1845-O 2,094,000
1846 2,210,000
1846-O Medium Date 2,304,000
1847 1,156,000
1847-O 2,584,000
1848 580,000
1848-O 3,180,000
1849 1,252,000
1849-O 2,310,000
1850 227,000
1850-O 2,456,000
1851 200,750
1851-O 402,000
1852 77,130
1852-O 144,000
1853-O 4 Known

Arrows at Date, Rays Around Eagle
1853 3,532,708
1853-O 1,328,000

Arrows at Date, No Rays
1854 2,982,000
1854-O 5,240,000
1855 759,500
1855-O 3,688,000
1855-S 129,950

No Motto Above Eagle

1856 938,000
1856-O 2,658,000
1856-S 211,000
1857 1,988,000
1857-O 818,000
1857-S 158,000
1858 4,226,000
1858-O 7,294,000
1858-S 476,000
1859 747,200
1859-O 2,834,000
1859-S 566,000
1860 302,700
1860-O 1,290,000
1860-S 472,000
1861 2,887,400
1861-O 2,532,633
1861-S 939,500
1862 253,000
1862-S 1,352,000
1863 503,200
1863-S 916,000
1864 379,100
1864-S 658,000
1865 511,400
1865-S 675,000
1866-S No Motto 60,000

The Liberty Seated half dollar coin was designed by sculptor and engraver Christian Gobrecht.

- **Years of minting:** 1839-1891
- **Silver:** 0.36169 troy oz
- **Value:** 50 cents (0.50 US dollars)
- **Diameter:** 30.6 mm
- **Composition:** 90% silver, 10% copper
- **Edge:** reeded
- **Thickness:** 1.8 mm
- **Weight:** 13.36g, 12.44g

Coin Mintages
Liberty Seated Half Dollar Mintage

Motto Above Eagle

1866 744,900
1866-S 994,000
1867 449,300
1867-S 1,196,000
1868 417,600
1868-S 1,160,000
1869 795,300
1869-S 656,000
1870 633,900
1870-CC 54,617
1870-S 1,004,000
1871 1,203,600
1871-CC 153,950
1871-S 2,178,000
1872 880,600
1872-CC 257,000
1872-S 580,000
1873 Close 3 587,000
1873 Open 3 214,200
1873-CC 122,500
1873-S No Arrows 5,000

Arrows at Date

1873 1,815,150
1873-CC 214,560
1873-S 228,000
1874 2,359,600
1874-CC 59,000
1874-S 394,000

Motto Above Eagle

1875 6,026,800
1875-CC 1,008,000
1875-S 3,200,000
1876 8,418,000
1876-CC 1,956,000
1876-S 4,528,000
1877 8,304,000
1877-CC 1,420,000
1877-S 5,356,000
1878 1,377,600
1878-CC 62,000
1878-S 12,000
1879 4,800
1880 8,400
1881 10,000
1882 4,400
1883 8,000
1884 4,400
1885 5,200
1886 5,000
1887 5,000
1888 12,001
1889 12,000
1890 12,000
1891 200,000

Coin Mintages

Barber Half Dollar Mintage

1892 934,000	1903 2,278,000
1892 Proof 1,245	1903 Proof 755
1892-O 390,000	1903-O 2,100,000
1892-S 1,029,028	1903-S 1,920,772
1893 1,826,000	1904 2,992,000
1893 Proof 792	1904 Proof 670
1893-O 1,389,000	1904-O 1,117,600
1893-S 740,000	1904-S 553,038
1894 1,148,000	1905 662,000
1894 Proof 972	1905 Proof 727
1894-O 2,138,000	1905-O 505,000
1894-S 4,048,960	1905-S 2,494,000
1895 1,834,338	1906 2,638,000
1895 Proof 880	1906 Proof 675
1895-O 1,766,000	1906-D 4,028,000
1895-S 1,108,086	1906-O 2,446,000
1896 950,000	1906-S 1,740,154
1896 Proof 762	1907 2,598,000
1896-O 924,000	1907 Proof 575
1896-S 1,140,948	1907-D 3,856,000
1897 2,480,000	1907-O 3,946,000
1897 Proof 731	1907-S 1,250,000
1897-O 632,000	1908 1,354,000
1897-S 933,900	1908 Proof 545
1898 2,956,000	1908-D 3,280,000
1898 Proof 735	1908-O 5,360,000
1898-O 874,000	1908-S 1,644,828
1898-S 2,358,550	1909 2,368,000
1899 5,538,000	1909 Proof 650
1899 Proof 846	1909-O 925,400
1899-O 1,724,000	1909-S 1,764,000
1899-S 1,686,411	1910 418,000
1900 4,762,000	1910 Proof 551
1900 Proof 912	1910-S 1,948,000
1900-O 2,744,000	1911 1,406,000
1900-S 2,560,322	1911 Proof 543
1901 4,268,000	1911-D 695,080
1901 Proof 813	1911-S 1,272,000
1901-O 1,124,000	1912 1,550,000
1901-S 847,044	1912 Proof 700
1902 4,922,000	1912-D 2,300,800
1902 Proof 777	1912-S 1,370,000
1902-O 2,526,000	1913 188,000
1902-S 1,460,670	1913 Proof 627

The Barber half dollar coin was designed by sculptor and engraver Charles E. Barber.

- **Years of minting:** 1891-1916
- **Silver:** 0.36169 troy oz
- **Value:** 50 cents (0.50 US dollars)
- **Diameter:** 30.6 mm
- **Composition:** 90% silver, 10% copper
- **Edge:** reeded
- **Thickness:** 1.8 mm
- **Weight:** 12.50 grams

1913-D 534,000
1913-S 604,000
1914 124,230
1914 Proof 380
1914-S 992,000
1915 138,000
1915 Proof 450
1915-D 1,170,400
1915-S 1,604,000

Coin Mintages

Walking Liberty Half Dollar Mintage

1916	608,000
1916 D	1,014,400
1916-S	**508,000**
1917	2,292,000
1917 D Obv Mint Mark	
765,400	
1917 D Rev Mint Mark	
1,940,000	
1917 S Obv Mint Mark	
952,000	
1917 S Rev Mint Mark	
5,554,000	
1918	6,634,000
1918 D	3,853,040
1918 S	10,282,000
1919	**962,000**
1919 D	1,165,000
1919 S	1,552,000
1920	6,372,000
1920 D	1,551,000
1920 S	4,624,000
1921	**246,000**
1921 D	**208,000**
1921 S	**548,000**
1923 S	2,178,000
1927 S	2,392,000
1928 S	1,940,000
1929 D	1,001,200
1929 S	1,902,000
1933 S	1,786,000
1934	6,964,000
1934 D	2,361,400
1934 S	3,652,000
1935	9,162,000
1935 D	3,003,800
1935 S	3,854,000
1936	12,614,000
1936 D	4,252,400
1936 S	3,884,000
1937	9,522,000
1937 D	1,676,000
1937 S	2,090,000
1938	4,110,000
1938 D	**491,600**
1939	6,812,000
1939 D	4,267,800
1939 S	2,552,000
1940	9,156,000
1940 S	4,550,000
1941	24,192,000
1941 D	11,248,400
1941 S	8,098,000
1942	47,818,000
1942 D	10,973,800
1942 S	12,708,000
1943	53,190,000
1943 D	11,346,000
1943 S	13,450,000
1944	28,206,000
1944 D	9,769,000
1944 S	8,904,000
1945	31,502,000
1945 D	9,966,800
1945 S	10,156,000
1946	12,118,000
1946 D	2,151,000
1946 S	3,724,000
1947	4,094,000
1947 D	3,900,600

The Walking Liberty half dollar coin was designed by sculptor and engraver Adolph A. Weinman.

- **Years of minting:** 1916–1947
- **Silver:** 0.36169 troy oz
- **Value:** 50 cents (0.50 US dollars)
- **Diameter:** 30.63 mm
- **Composition:** 90% silver, 10% copper
- **Edge:** reeded
- **Thickness:** 1.8 mm
- **Weight:** 12.50 grams

Key Dates (Under 1 Million Mintage)
1916
1916 S
1917 D Obv Mint Mark
1917 S Obv Mint Mark
1919
1921
1921 D
1921 S
1938 D

Coin Mintages

Franklin Half Dollar Mintage

Year	Mintage
1948	**3,006,814**
1948 D	4,028,600
1949	5,614,000
1949 D	4,120,600
1949 S	**3,744,000**
1950	7,742,123
1950 D	8,031,600
1951	16,802,102
1951 D	9,475,200
1951 S	13,696,000
1952	21,192,093
1952 D	25,395,600
1952 S	5,526,000
1953	**2,668,120**
1953 D	20,900,400
1953 S	4,148,000
1954	13,188,202
1954 D	25,445,580
1954 S	4,993,400
1955	**2,498,181**
1956	4,032,000
1957	5,114,000
1957 D	19,966,850
1958	4,042,000
1958 D	23,962,412
1959	6,200,000
1959 D	13,053,750
1960	6,024,000
1960 D	18,215,812
1961	8,290,000
1961 D	20,276,442
1962	9,714,000
1962 D	35,473,281
1963	22,164,000
1963 D	67,069,292

Key Dates
1948
1949 S
1953
1955

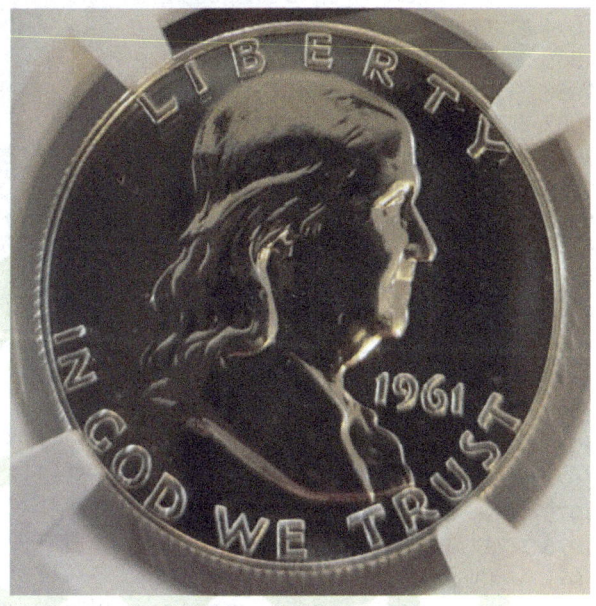

Image: Justin Couch

The Franklin half dollar coin was designed by Chief engraver John R. Sinnock.

- **Years of minting:** 1948–1963
- **Silver:** 0.36169 troy oz
- **Value:** 50 cents (0.50 US dollars)
- **Composition:** 90% silver, 10% copper
- **Diameter:** 30.61 mm (1.21 in)
- **Edge:** reeded
- **Weight:** 12.50 grams

Coin Mintages

Kennedy Half Dollar Mintage

Year	Mintage	Year	Mintage
1964	273,304,004	1989 D	23,000,216
1964 D	156,205,446	1990	22,278,000
1965	65,879,366	1990 D	20,096,242
1966	108,984,932	1991	14,874,000
1967	295,046,978	1991 D	15,054,678
1968 D	246,951,930	1992	17,628,000
1969 D	129,881,800	1992 D	17,000,106
1970 D	**2,150,000**	1993	15,510,000
1971	155,164,000	1993-D	15,000,006
1971 D	302,097,424	1994	23,718,000
1972	153,180,000	1994 D	23,828,110
1972 D	141,890,000	1995	26,496,000
1973	64,964,000	1995 D	26,288,000
1973 D	83,171,400	1996	24,442,000
1974	201,596,000	1996 D	24,744,000
1974 D	79,066,300	1997	20,882,000
1976	234,308,000	1997 D	19,876,000
1976 D	287,565,248	1998	15,646,000
1977	43,598,000	1998 D	15,064,000
1977 D	31,449,106	1999	8,900,000
1978	14,350,000	1999 D	10,682,000
1978 D	13,765,799	2000	22,600,000
1979	68,312,000	2000 D	19,466,000
1979 D	15,815,422	2001	21,200,000
1980	44,134,000	2001 D	19,504,000
1980 D	33,456,449	**2002**	**3,100,000**
1981	29,544,000	**2002-D**	**2,500,000**
1981 D	27,839,533	**2003**	**2,500,000**
1982	10,819,000	**2003 D**	**2,500,000**
1982 D	13,140,102	**2004**	**2,900,000**
1983	34,139,000	**2004 D**	**2,900,000**
1983 D	32,472,244	**2005**	**3,800,000**
1984	26,029,000	**2005 D**	**3,500,000**
1984 D	26,262,158	**2006**	**2,400,000**
1985	18,706,962	**2006 D**	**2,000,000**
1985 D	19,814,034	**2007**	**2,400,000**
1986	13,107,633	**2007 D**	**2,400,000**
1986 D	15,336,145	**2008**	**1,700,000**
1987	**2,890,758**	**2008 D**	**1,700,000**
1987 D	**2,890,758**	**2009**	**1,900,000**
1988	13,626,000	**2009 D**	**1,900,000**
1988 D	12,000,096	**2010**	**1,800,000**
1989	24,542,000	**2010 D**	**1,700,000**

The Kennedy half dollar coin was intended as a memorial for President John F. Kennedy after his assassination. The coin was designed by Mint sculptors Gilroy Roberts and Frank Gasparro.

- **Years of minting:** 1964–present
- **Value:** 50 cents (.50 US dollar)
- **Diameter:** 30.6 mm
- **Thickness:** 2.15 mm
- **Edge:** reeded
- **Weight:** Copper-nickel clad: 11.34 grams, 40% Silver clad: 11.50 grams, 90% Silver: 12.50 grams, 2014 Gold: 23.33 grams

<u>Key Dates</u>
1970 D
1987
1987 D
2002 - 2022 NIFC's
(Not intended for circulation)

Coin Mintages

Kennedy Half Dollar Mintage

2011-P 1,750,000
2011-D 1,700,000
2012-P 1,800,000
2012-D 1,700,000
2013-P 5,000,000
2013-D 4,600,000
2014-P 2,500,000
2014-P High Relief* 197,608
2014-D 2,100,000
2014-D High Relief* 197,608
2014-D Silver 219,173
2014-S Silver Enhanced Uncirculated 219,173
2015-P 2,300,000
2015-D 2,300,000
2016-P 2,100,000
2016-D 2,100,000
2017-P 1,800,000
2017-D 2,900,000
2018-P 4,800,000
2018-D 6,100,000
2019-P 1,700,000
2019-D 1,700,000
2020-P 5,400,000
2020-D 7,700,000
2021-P 2,300,000
2021-D 3,400,000
2022-P 4,900,000
2022-D 4,800,000
2023-P 30,200,000
2023-D 27,800,000

Look for a doubled die obverse on the 1974 Kennedy Half Dollar coin. Visible doubling can be seen on the lettering as well as the date itself.

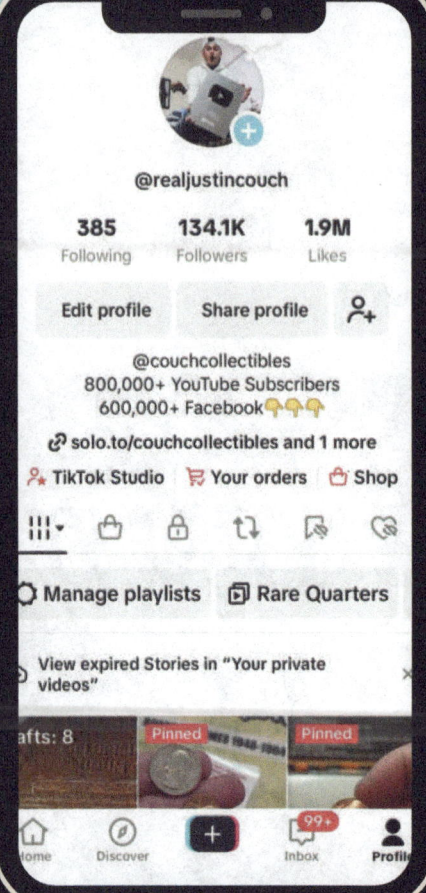

100,000+ FOLLOWERS!

DAILY
COIN VIDEOS AND LIVE STREAMS ON TIKTOK!

@REALJUSTINCOUCH

FOLLOW COUCH COLLECTIBLES IT'S FREE!

SCAN ME

Coin Mintages
Liberty Seated Dollar Mintage

1840 61,005	1868 162,100
1841 173,000	1868 Proof 600
1842 184,618	1869 423,700
1843 165,100	1869 Proof 600
1844 20,000	1870 415,000
1845 24,500	1870 Proof 1,000
1846 110,600	1870-CC 11,758
1846-O 59,000	1870-S 12 Estimated
1847 140,750	1871 1,073,800
1848 15,000	1871 Proof 960
1849 62,600	1871-CC 1,376
1850 7,500	1872 1,105,500
1850-O 40,000	1872 Proof 950
1851 1,300	1872-CC 3,150
1852 1,100	1872-S 9,000
1853 46,110	1873 293,000
1854 33,140	1873 Proof 600
1855 26,000	1873-CC 2,300
1856 63,500	1873-S 700
1857 94,000	
1858 Proof 210	
1859 255,700	
1859 Proof 800	
1859-O 360,000	
1859-S 20,000	
1860 217,600	
1860 Proof 1,330	
1860-O 515,000	
1861 77,500	
1861 Proof 1,000	
1862 11,540	
1862 Proof 550	
1863 27,200	
1863 Proof 460	
1864 30,700	
1864 Proof 470	
1865 46,500	
1865 Proof 500	
1866 48,900	
1866 Proof 725	
1866 No Motto 2 Known	
1867 46,900	
1867 Proof 625	

The silver Liberty Seated Dollar coin was designed by chief engraver, Christian Gobrecht.

- **Years of minting:** 1840-1873
- **Value:** $1 (One US dollar)
- **Diameter:** 38.1 mm
- **Mass:** 26.73 grams
- **Edge:** reeded
- **Composition:** 90% silver, 10% copper
- **Silver:** 0.77344 troy oz
- **Mint marks:** O, S, CC. Located under the eagle on reverse. Philadelphia Mint examples do not have a mint mark.

Coin Mintages

Morgan Dollar Mintage

1878 8TF	749,500	1889 O	11,875,000
1878 7TF	9,759,300	**1889 S**	**700,000**
1878 CC	2,212,000	1890	16,802,000
1878 S	9,774,000	1890 CC	2,309,041
1879	14,806,000	1890 O	10,701,000
1879 CC	**756,000**	1890 S	8,230,373
1879 O	2,887,000	1891	8,693,556
1879 S	9,110,000	1891 CC	1,618,000
1880	12,600,000	1891 O	7,954,529
1880 CC	**591,000**	1891 S	5,296,000
1880 O	5,305,000	1892	1,036,000
1880 S	8,900,000	1892 CC	1,352,000
1881	9,163,000	1892 O	2,744,000
1881 CC	**296,000**	1892 S	1,200,000
1881 O	5,708,000	**1893**	**378,000**
1881 S	12,760,000	**1893 CC**	**677,000**
1882	11,100,000	**1893 O**	**300,000**
1882 CC	1,133,000	**1893 S**	**100,000**
1882 O	6,090,000	**1894**	**110,000**
1882 S	9,250,000	1894 O	1,723,000
1883	12,290,000	1894 S	1,260,000
1883 CC	1,204,000	**1895 O**	**450,000**
1883 O	8,725,000	**1895 S**	**400,000**
1883 S	6,250,000	1896	9,976,000
1884	14,070,000	1896 O	4,900,000
1884 CC	1,136,000	1896 S	5,000,000
1884 O	9,730,000	1897	2,822,000
1884 S	3,200,000	1897 O	4,004,000
1885	17,787,000	1897 S	5,825,000
1885 CC	**238,000**	1898	5,884,000
1885 O	9,185,000	1898 O	4,440,000
1885 S	1,497,000	1898 S	4,102,000
1886	19,963,000	**1899**	**330,000**
1886 O	10,710,000	1899 O	12,290,000
1886 S	**750,000**	1899 S	2,562,000
1887	20,290,000	1900	8,830,000
1887 O	11,550,000	1900 O	12,590,000
1887 S	1,771,000	1900 S	3,540,000
1888	19,183,000	1901	6,962,000
1888 O	12,150,000	1901 O	13,320,000
1888 S	**657,000**	1901 S	2,284,000
1889	21,726,000	1902	7,994,000
1889 CC	**350,000**	1902 O	8,636,000
1902 S	1,530,000		
1903	4,652,000		
1903 O	4,450,000		
1903 S	1,241,000		
1904	2,788,000		
1904 O	3,720,000		
1904 S	2,304,000		
1921	44,690,000		
1921 D	20,345,000		
1921 S	21,695,000		

The silver Morgan Dollar was designed by United States Mint Assistant Engraver George T. Morgan.

- **Years of minting:** 1878-1904, 1921, 2021-2024
- **Mint marks:** None (Philadelphia), CC (Carson City), S (San Francisco), O (New Orleans), D (Denver)
- **Diameter:** 38.1 mm (1.5 in)
- **Value:** $1 United States dollar
- **Composition:** 90.0% Silver, 10.0% Copper, (2021-Present .999 Silver)
- **Thickness:** 2.4 mm (0.09 in)
- **Edge:** reeded
- **Weight:** 26.73 grams

Key Dates
Under 1 million mintage dates are highlighted in bold text.

Coin Mintages

Modern Morgan Dollar Mintages

2021 174,854
2021-CC Privy Mark 173,798
2021-D 174,715
2021-O Privy Mark 173,551
2021-S 174,879
2023 273,727
2023-S Proof 378,956
2023-S Reverse Proof 247,820
2024 175,240
2024-S Proof 180,963
2024-S Reverse Proof 143,629

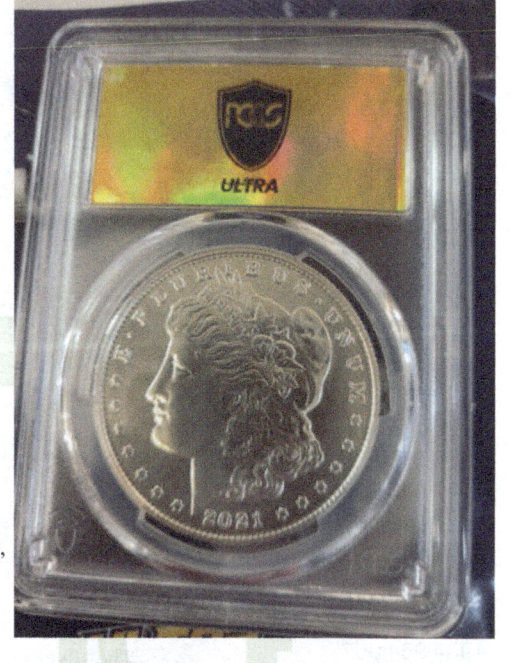

The silver Morgan Dollar was designed by United States Mint Assistant Engraver George T. Morgan.

- **Years of minting:** 1878-1904, 1921, 2021-2024
- **Mint marks:** None (Philadelphia), CC (Carson City), S (San Francisco), O (New Orleans), D (Denver)
- **Diameter:** 38.1 mm (1.5 in)
- **Value:** $1 United States dollar
- **Composition:** 90.0% Silver, 10.0% Copper, (2021-Present .999 Silver)
- **Thickness:** 2.4 mm (0.09 in)
- **Edge:** reeded
- **Weight:** 26.73 grams

Coin Mintages

Peace Dollar Mintage

1921 High Relief 1,006,473
1922 High Relief 35,401
1922 51,737,000
1922-D 15,063,000
1922-S 17,475,000
1923 30,800,000
1923-D 6,811,000
1923-S 19,020,000
1924 11,811,000
1924-S 1,728,000
1925 10,198,000
1925-S 1,610,000
1926 1,939,000
1926-D 2,348,700
1926-S 6,980,000
1927 848,000
1927-D 1,268,900
1927-S 866,000
1928 360,649
1928-S 1,632,000
1934 954,057
1934-D 1,569,500
1934-S 1,011,000
1935 1,576,000
1935-S 1,964,000

2021 199,940
2023 273,969
2023-S Proof 344,244
2023-S Reverse Proof 247,820
2024 167,509
2024-S Proof 165,075
2024-S Reverse Proof 143,629

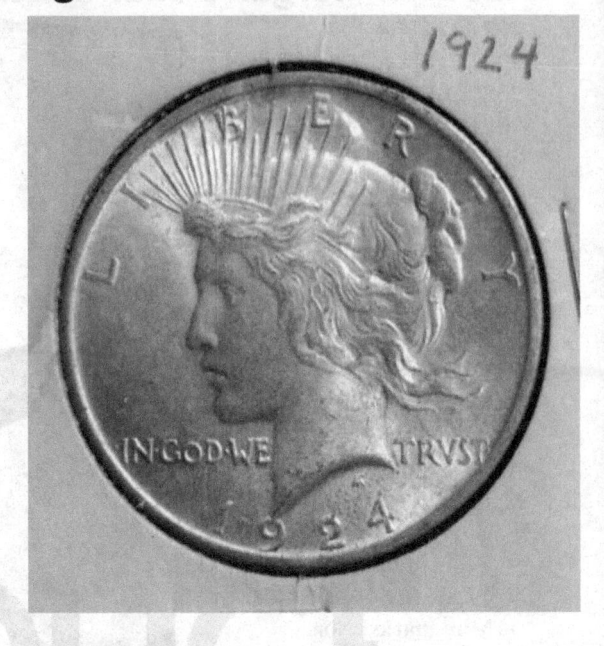

The silver Peace Dollar was designed by italian-American sculptor Anthony de Francisci.

- **Years of minting:** 1921-1935, 2021-2024
- **Mint marks:** None (Philadelphia), S (San Francisco), D (Denver)
- **Diameter:** 38.1 mm (1.5 in)
- **Value:** $1 United States dollar
- **Composition:** 90.0% Silver, 10.0% Copper, (2021-Present .999 Silver)
- **Thickness:** 2.4 mm (0.09 in)
- **Edge:** reeded
- **Weight:** 26.73 grams

Coin Mintages
Eisenhower Dollar Mintage

Year	Mintage
1971	47,799,000
1971 D	68,587,424
1971 S Silver	6,868,530
1972	75,890,000
1972 D	92,548,511
1972 S Silver	2,193,056
1973	**1,769,258**
1973 D	**1,769,258**
1973 S Silver	**1,883,140**
1974	27,366,000
1974 D	45,517,000
1974 S Silver	**1,900,156**
1976 Type 1	4,019,000
1976 D Type 1	21,048,710
1976 Type 2	113,318,000
1976 D Type 2	82,179,564
1976 S Silver	4,908,319
1977	12,596,000
1977 D	32,983,006
1978	25,702,000
1978 D	33,102,890

Key Dates
1973
1973 D
1973 S Silver
1974 S Silver

The Eisenhower dollar coin was designed by Frank Gasparro.

- **Years of minting:** 1971–1978. Coins struck in 1975 and 1976 bear double date "1776–1976"
- **Value:** $1 U.S. dollar
- **Diameter:** 38.1 mm (1.5 in)
- **Edge:** reeded
- **Thickness:** 2.58 mm (0.1 in)
- **Weight:** Copper/nickel-clad: 22.68 grams, Silver clad: 24.624 grams

Coin Mintages
Susan B. Anthony Dollar Mintage

1979 P		360,222,000
1979 D		288,015,744
1979 S		109,576,000
1979 S	Proof	3,677,175
1980 P		27,610,000
1980 D		41,628,708
1980 S		20,422,000
1980 S	Proof	3,544,806
1981 P		3,000,000
1981 D		3,250,000
1981 S		3,492,000
1981 S	Proof	4,063,083
1999 P		29,592,000
1999 D		11,776,000
1999 S	**Proof**	**750,000**

Key Dates
1999 S Proof

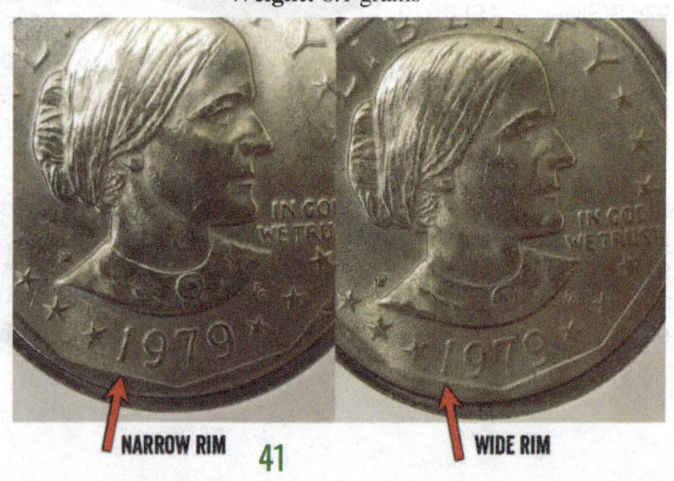

The Susan B. Anthony dollar coin was designed by Frank Gasparro, the Chief Engraver of the United States Mint. In the image below you will see the "narrow rim vs. wide rim" dollar coin. The wide rim is the more scarce of two.

- **Years of minting:** 1979–1981, 1999
- **Value:** $1 U.S. dollar
- **Mint marks:** P (Philadelphia Mint), D (Denver Mint), S (San Francisco Mint)
- **Composition:** 75% copper, 25% nickel, clad to pure copper core
- **Diameter:** 26.5 mm (1.04 in)
- **Edge:** reeded
- **Thickness:** 2.00 mm (0.08 in)
- **Weight:** 8.1 grams

NARROW RIM — WIDE RIM

Coin Mintages

Sacagawea Dollar Mintages

2000-P 767,140,000
2000-D 518,916,000
2001-P 62,468,000
2001-D 70,939,500
2002-P 3,865,610
2002-D 3,732,000
2003-P 3,080,000
2003-D 3,080,000
2004-P 2,660,000
2004-D 2,660,000
2005-P 2,520,000
2005-D 2,520,000
2006-P 4,900,000
2006-D 2,800,000
2007-P 3,640,000
2007-D 3,920,000
2008-P 1,820,000
2008-D 1,820,000
2009-P 39,200,000
2009-D 35,700,000
2010-P 32,060,000
2010-D 48,720,000
2011-P 29,400,000
2011-D 48,160,000
2012-P 2,800,000
2012-D 3,080,000
2013-P 1,820,000
2013-D 1,820,000
2014-P 3,080,000
2014-D 2,800,000
2014-D Enhanced Uncirculated* 50,000
2015-P 2,800,000
2015-D 2,240,000
2015-W Enhanced Uncirculated* 88,805
2016-P 2,800,000
2016-D 2,100,000
2016-S Enhanced Uncirculated* 57,737
2017-P 1,820,000
2017-D 1,540,000
2018-P 1,400,000
2018-D 1,400,000
2019-P 1,400,000
2019-P Enhanced Uncirculated 46,964
2019-D 1,540,000
2020-P 1,260,000
2020-D 1,260,000
2021-P 1,400,000
2021-D 1,260,000

The Sacagawea one dollar coin obverse was designed by Glenna Goodacre. From 2000 to 2008, the reverse of the coin was designed by Thomas D. Rogers.

- **Years of minting:** 2000-Present
- **Value:** $1 U.S. dollar
- **Mint marks:** P (Philadelphia), D (Denver), S (San Francisco), W (West Point, special strikings only)
- **Composition:** Core: 100% Cu, Cladding: 77% Cu, 12% Zn, 7% Mn, 4% Ni, Overall: 88.5% Cu, 6% Zn, 3.5% Mn, 2% Ni
- **Diameter:** 26.49 mm (1.043 in)
- **Edge:** Plain (2000–2008), Lettered (2009–present)
- **Thickness:** 2.00 mm (0.079 in)
- **Weight:** 8.100 g (0.26 troy oz)

Coin Mintages

Presidential Dollar Mintages

2007-P George Washington 176,680,000
2007-D George Washington 163,680,000
2007-S Proof George Washington 3,965,989
2007-P John Adams 112,420,000
2007-D John Adams 112,140,000
2007-S Proof John Adams 3,965,989
2007-P Thomas Jefferson 100,800,000
2007-D Thomas Jefferson 102,810,000
2007-S Proof Thomas Jefferson 3,965,989
2007-P James Madison 84,560,000
2007-D James Madison 87,780,000
2007-S Proof James Madison 3,965,989
2008-P James Monroe 64,260,000
2008-D James Monroe 60,230,000
2008-S Proof James Monroe 3,083,940
2008-P John Quincy Adams 57,540,000
2008-D John Quincy Adams 57,720,000
2008-S Proof John Quincy Adams 3,083,940
2008-P Andrew Jackson 61,180,000
2008-D Andrew Jackson 61,070,000
2008-S Proof Andrew Jackson 3,083,940
2008-P Martin Van Buren 51,520,000
2008-D Martin Van Buren 50,960,000
2008-S Proof Martin Van Buren 3,083,940
2009-P William Henry Harrison 43,260,000
2009-D William Henry Harrison 55,160,000
2009-S Proof William Henry Harrison 2,809,452
2009-P John Tyler 43,540,000
2009-D John Tyler 43,540,000
2009-S Proof John Tyler 2,809,452
2009-P James K. Polk 46,620,000
2009-D James K. Polk 41,720,000
2009-S Proof James K. Polk 2,809,452
2009-P Zachary Taylor 41,580,000
2009-D Zachary Taylor 36,680,000
2009-S Proof Zachary Taylor 2,809,452

The Presidential one dollar coin was designed by Don Everhart.

- **Years of minting:** 2007–2011 (Circulation), 2012–2016; 2020 (Collectors Only)
- **Value:** $1 U.S. dollar
- **Composition:** Copper with manganese brass cladding: 88.5% Cu, 6% Zn, 3.5% Mn, 2% Ni
- **Diameter:** 26.49 mm (1.043 in)
- **Edge:** Engraved: lettering "E pluribus unum", the coin's mint mark, its year of issue, and 13 five-pointed stars (prior to 2009: lettering "In God We Trust")
- **Thickness:** 2.00 mm (0.079 in)
- **Weight:** 8.100 g (0.26 troy oz)

Coin Mintages
Presidential Dollar Mintages

2011-P Andrew Johnson 35,560,000
2011-D Andrew Johnson 37,100,000
2011-S Proof Andrew Johnson 1,972,863
2011-P Ulysses S. Grant 38,080,000
2011-D Ulysses S. Grant 37,940,000
2011-S Proof Ulysses S. Grant 1,972,863
2011-P Rutherford B. Hayes 37,660,000
2011-D Rutherford B. Hayes 36,820,000
2011-S Proof Rutherford B. Hayes 1,972,863
2011-P James Garfield 37,100,000
2011-D James Garfield 37,100,000
2011-S Proof James Garfield 1,972,863
2012-P Chester Arthur 6,020,000
2012-D Chester Arthur 4,060,000
2012-S Proof Chester Arthur 1,438,743
2012-P Grover Cleveland (1st Term) 5,460,000
2012-D Grover Cleveland (1st Term) 4,060,000
2012-S Proof Grover Cleveland (1st Term) 1,438,743
2012-P Benjamin Harrison 5,640,000
2012-D Benjamin Harrison 4,200,000
2012-S Proof Benjamin Harrison 1,438,743
2012-P Grover Cleveland (2nd Term) 10,680,000
2012-D Grover Cleveland (2nd Term) 3,920,000
2013-P William McKinley 4,760,000
2013-D William McKinley 3,365,100
2013-S Proof William McKinley 1,488,798
2013-P Theodore Roosevelt 5,310,700
2013-D Theodore Roosevelt 3,920,000
2013-S Proof Theodore Roosevelt 1,503,943
2013-P William Howard Taft 4,760,000
2013-D William Howard Taft 3,360,000
2013 S Proof William Howard Taft 1,488,798
2013-P Woodrow Wilson 4,620,000
2013-D Woodrow Wilson 3,360,000
2013-S Proof Woodrow Wilson 1,488,798

Coin Mintages
Presidential Dollar Mintages

2014-P Warren G. Harding 6,160,000
2014-D Warren G. Harding 3,780,000
2014-S Proof Warren G. Harding 1,373,569
2014-P Calvin Coolidge 4,480,000
2014-D Calvin Coolidge 3,780,000
2014-S Proof Calvin Coolidge 1,373,569
2014-P Herbert Hoover 4,480,000
2014-D Herbert Hoover 3,780,000
2014-S Proof Herbert Hoover 1,373,569
2014-P Franklin D. Roosevelt 4,760,000
2014-D Franklin D. Roosevelt 3,920,000
2014-S Proof Franklin D. Roosevelt 1,392,619
2015-P Harry S. Truman 4,900,000
2015-P Reverse Proof Harry S. Truman 16,812
2015-D Harry S. Truman 3,500,000
2015-S Proof Harry S. Truman 1,272,232
2015-P Dwight D. Eisenhower 4,900,000
2015-P Reverse Proof Dwight D. Eisenhower 16,744
2015-D Dwight D. Eisenhower 3,645,998
2015-S Proof Dwight D. Eisenhower 1,272,232
2015-P John F. Kennedy 6,160,000
2015-P Reverse Proof John F. Kennedy 49,051
2015-D John F. Kennedy 5,180,000
2015-S Proof John F. Kennedy 1,272,232
2015-P Lyndon B. Johnson 7,840,000
2015-P Reverse Proof Lyndon B. Johnson 23,905
2015-D Lyndon B. Johnson 4,200,000
2015-S Proof Lyndon B. Johnson 1,272,232
2016-P Richard M. Nixon 5,460,000
2016-D Richard M. Nixon 4,340,000
2016-S Proof Richard M. Nixon 1,196,582
2016-P Gerald R. Ford 5,460,000
2016-D Gerald R. Ford 5,040,000
2016-S Proof Gerald R. Ford 1,196,582
2016-P Ronald Reagan 7,140,000
2016-D Ronald Reagan 5,880,000
2016-S Proof Ronald Reagan 1,196,582
2016-S Reverse Proof Ronald Reagan 47,447
2020-P George H.W. Bush 1,242,275
2020-D George H.W. Bush 1,502,425
2020-S Reverse Proof George H.W. Bush 11,251

20,000+ FOLLOWERS!

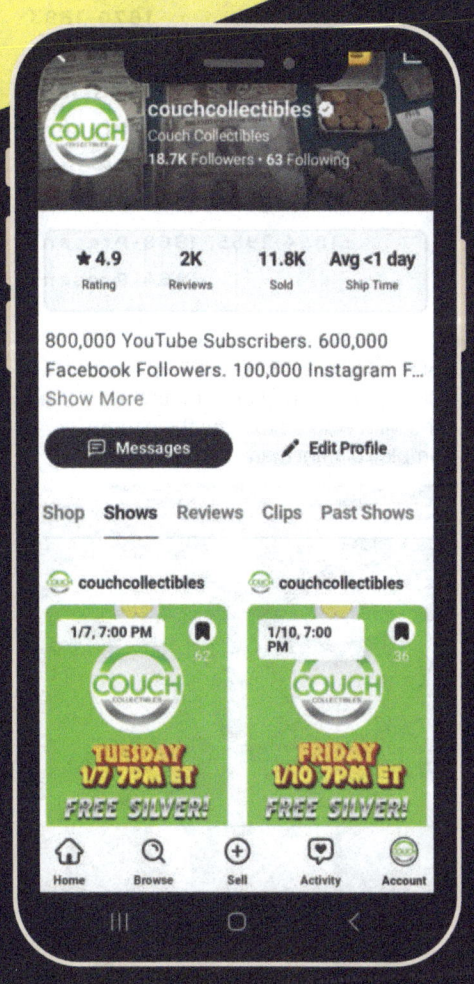

COUCH
COLLECTIBLES

FREE SILVER GIVEAWAYS ONLY ON WHATNOT!

@COUCHCOLLECTIBLES

whatnot

$15 FREE CREDIT FOR FIRST TIME USERS!

SCAN ME

Mint Marks

LOCATION	MINT MARK	YEARS USED
Carson City (NV)	CC	1870-1893
Charlotte (NC)	C	1838-1861
Dahlonega (GA)	D	1838-1861
Denver (CO)	D	1906-Present
New Orleans (LA)	O	1838-1861, 1879-1909
Philadelphia (PA)	P	1942-45, 1979-Present
San Francisco (CA)	S	1854-1955, 1968-Present
West Point (NY)	W	1984-Present

We'll look at the different placements of mint marks on coins over the years in the next few pages. Keep in mind that because of the Coinage Act of 1965, no mint marks appeared on circulating coins from 1965 to 1967. This was intentionally done to discourage people from collecting while the Mint worked to meet the country's coinage needs. Below are a few different examples of mint marks.

Washington Quarter

Morgan Dollar

Walking Liberty Half Dollar

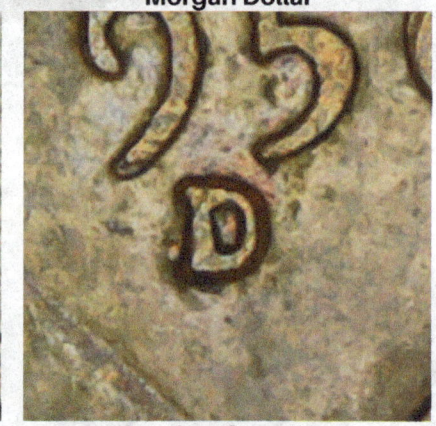

Lincoln Wheat Cent

Mint Marks
Indian Head Cent

Image: Justin Couch

You can find the "S" mint mark on the reverse of the Indian Head cent at the bottom of the coin. The only two Indian head cent dates that bear an "S" mint mark are the 1908 S and the 1909 S.

Here is an example of the very low minted 1908 S Indian head cent. This coin is apart of Bryan Hooper's coin collection. Thank you Bryan for being a long time subscriber and supporter of Couch Collectibles YouTube channel.

Images: Bryan Hooper Collection

48

Mint Marks
Lincoln Cent

Image: Justin Couch

You can find the P, D, or S mint mark on the obverse of the Lincoln cent under the date. The P mint mark was only used on the 2017 Lincoln Cent. All other Philadelphia minted cents did not have a mint mark. In 2019 the mint also produced a W mint mark proof Lincoln cent.

Mint Marks
Lincoln Cent

Image: Justin Couch

In 2019 the mint produced a 2019 W mint mark proof penny. Also below is a 2017 Lincoln cent with the P mint mark.

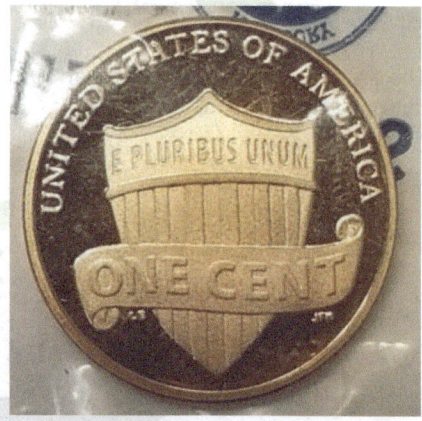

50

Mint Marks
Silver Three Cent Piece

Image courtesy of Professional Coin Grading Service (pcgs.com)

The silver three cent piece beared an "O" mint mark for only one year in 1851. All other dates did not a have mint mark.

Mint Marks
Liberty Head V Nickel

Image courtesy of Professional Coin Grading Service (pcgs.com)

You can find the mint mark on your Liberty Head V Nickels on the reverse of the coin at the bottom left under the dot. You will either see no mint mark (Philadelphia mint), a "D" mint mark (Denver mint) or an "S" mint mark in which represents the San Francisco mint.

Mint Marks
Buffalo Nickel

Image: Justin Couch

You will notice the Buffalo Nickel will have either no mint mark, a "D" mint mark, or an "S" mint mark. The mint mark will be located on the reverse of the coin under the words "Five Cents".

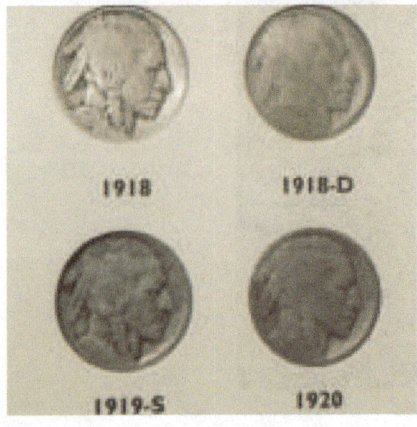

53

Mint Marks
Jefferson Nickel

Image: Justin Couch

The Jefferson nickel mint mark locations vary by date. Here are a few different examples of where those mint marks are located. Some will be on the obverse and others on the reverse of the coin. We'll look at silver nickels that have different mint mark placement as well.

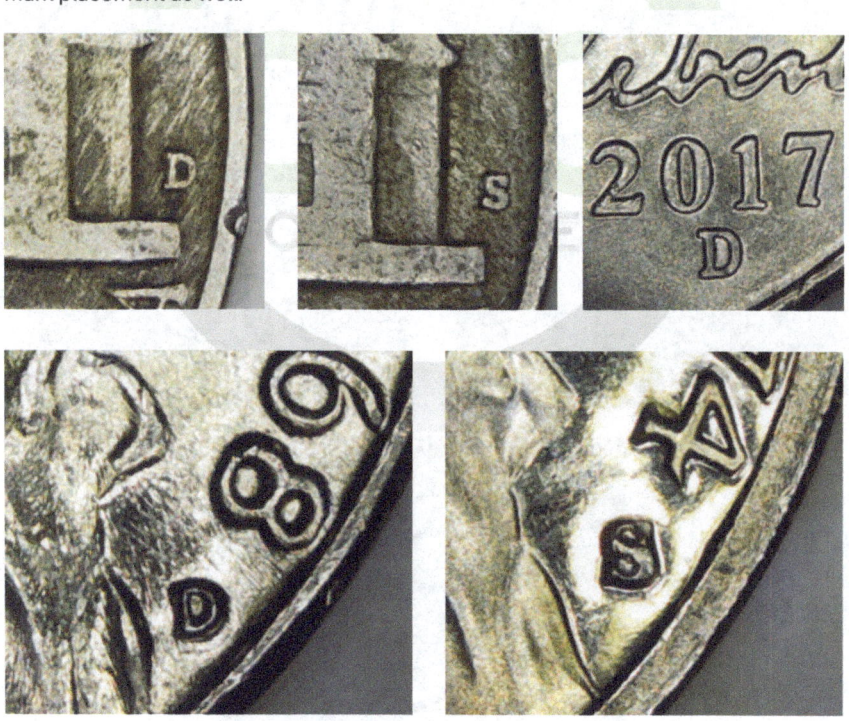

54

Mint Marks

Jefferson Nickel (1942-1945) 35% Silver

Image: Justin Couch

If you have a large mint mark on the reverse of your Jefferson nickel like the mint marks in the images below, you have a 35% silver nickel. This mint mark was only used from 1942-1945. Keep in mind there are both non-silver and silver nickels for the year 1942. Only the 1942 with these large mint marks are 35% silver coins.

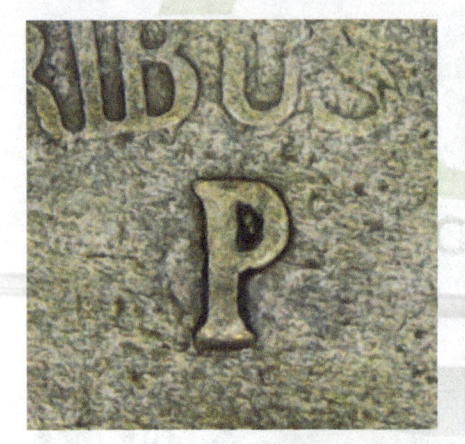

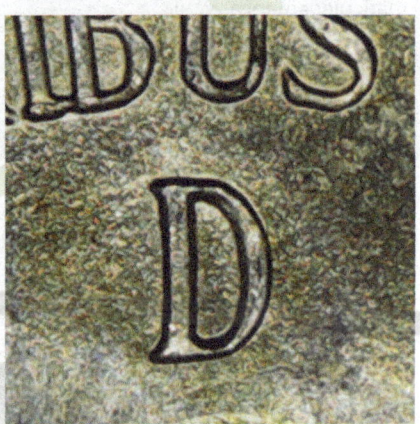

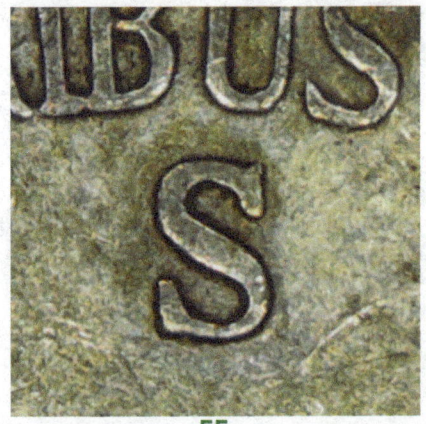

Mint Marks
Liberty Seated Dime

Image courtesy of Professional Coin Grading Service (pcgs.com)

The Liberty Seated silver dime will either have an "O", "S", "CC" or no mint mark on the reverse of the coin. You'll notice the placement of the "O" mint mark is different from the other mint marks.

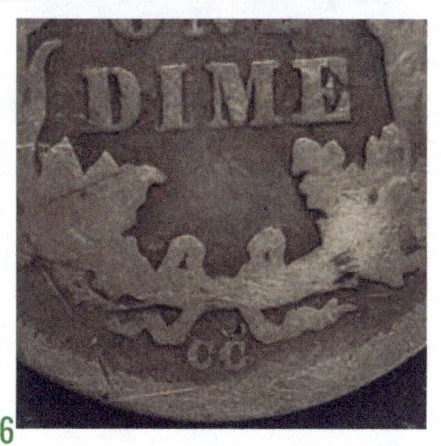

Mint Marks
Barber Dime

Image courtesy of Professional Coin Grading Service (pcgs.com)

The silver Barber dime will either have no mint mark, a "D", "S" or "O" mint mark on reverse of the coin at the bottom under the bow.

Mint Marks

Mercury Dime

Image: Justin Couch

For the Mercury dime, you will find the mint mark on the reverse of the coin at the bottom, to the right of the "E" in the word "one". There will be coins with no mint mark also. We'll look at a list of re-punched mint marks and other errors to look for on your silver dimes later in this book.

1945   1945-D   1945-S

Mint Marks
Roosevelt Dime

Image: Justin Couch

The mint mark placements on the Roosevelt dime vary by date. You can find the P, D, and "S" mint marks on the obverse of the coins. The "D" and "S" mint marks were also placed on the reverse of these coins. Some dates did not have mint marks.

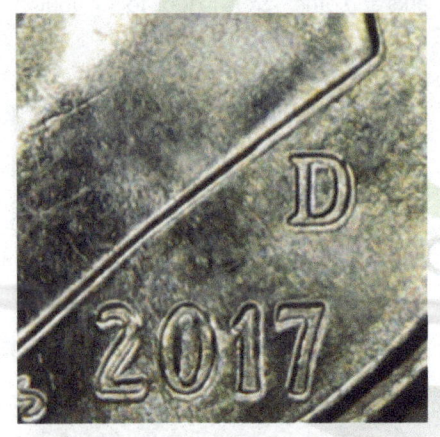

59

Mint Marks
Seated Liberty Quarter

Image courtesy of Professional Coin Grading Service (pcgs.com)

The silver Seated Liberty quarter dollar coin will have either no mint mark at all, an "S", "O" or "CC" mint mark on reverse of the coin at the bottom under the eagle.

Mint Marks

Barber Quarter

Image courtesy of Professional Coin Grading Service (pcgs.com)

The silver Barber quarter will have either no mint mark, a "D", "S", or "O" mint mark which can be seen at the bottom of the coin on the reverse under the eagle.

Mint Marks
Standing Liberty Quarter

The silver Standing Liberty Quarter was minted at all three mints in Philadelphia, Denver, and San Francisco. You will see no mint mark on the Philadelphia quarters, a "D" mint mark on the Denver minted quarters and an "S" mint mark on the San Francisco minted quarters. The mint mark is too the left of the date next to a star.

62

Mint Marks
Washington Quarter

Washington quarters have different placements of mint marks for different dates. Some will be on the obverse and others on the reverse. These quarters will have no mint marks, as well as P, D, S, and W mint marks. Remember from 1965-1967 these coins had no mint marks at all.

Mint Marks

Seated Liberty Half Dollar

Image courtesy of Professional Coin Grading Service (pcgs.com)

The silver Liberty Seated half dollar coin will have either no mint mark, an "S", or "O" mint mark on the reverse of the coin beneath the eagle at the bottom of the coin.

Mint Marks

Barber Half Dollar

Image courtesy of Professional Coin Grading Service (pcgs.com)

The silver Barber half dollar coin will either have no mint mark at all, a "D", "S", or an "O" mint mark at the bottom of the coin on the reverse beneath the eagle.

Mint Marks
Walking Liberty Half Dollar

Image: Justin Couch

You can find the "D" or "S" mint mark on the reverse of the Walking Liberty half dollar coin. For the 1917 half dollar, you'll notice they'll either have mint marks on the obverse or the reverse of the coin. The bottom images show you both the "D" and "S" mint marks on the reverse as well as on the obverse. Refer to the coin mintage page to see how many they produced of each coin.

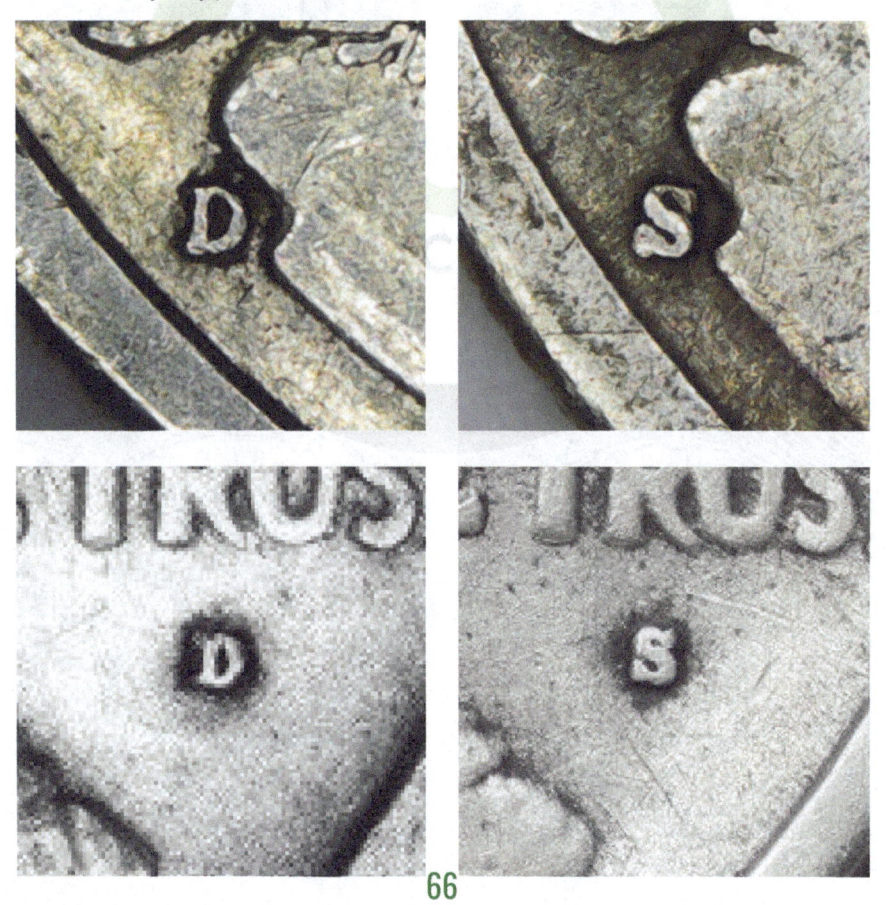

66

Mint Marks

Franklin Half Dollar

The Franklin half dollar coins will either have no mint mark, a "D" mint mark, or an "S" mint mark located on the reverse of the coin above the bell. *Image: ae_coins Instagram*

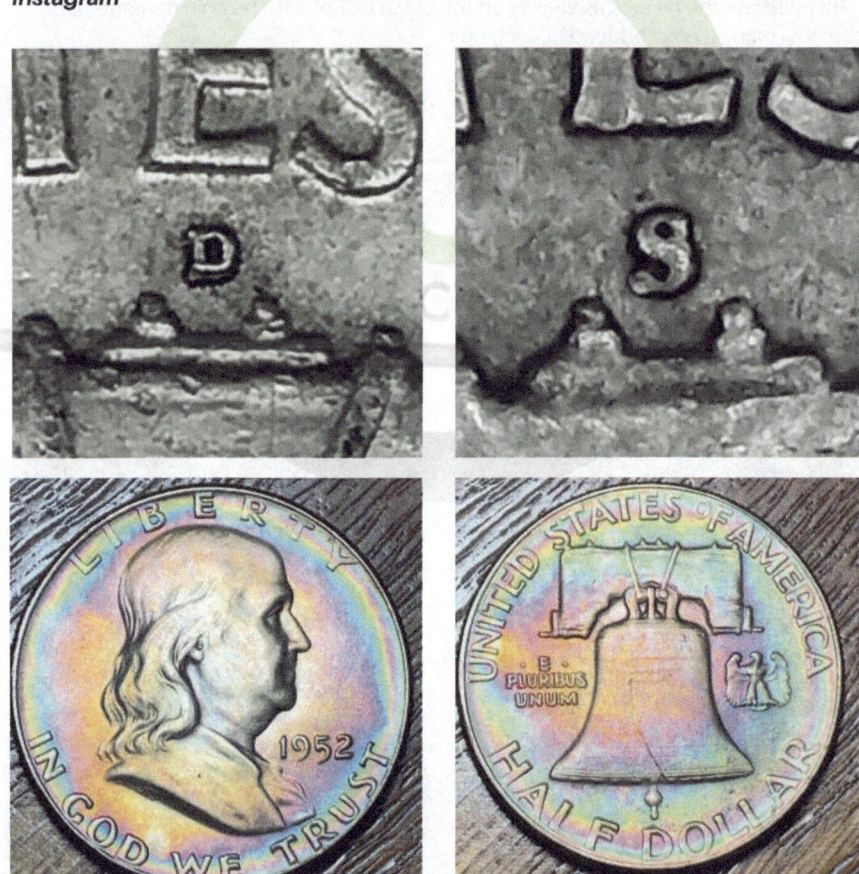

Mint Marks
Kennedy Half Dollar

KENNEDY HALF DOLLARS

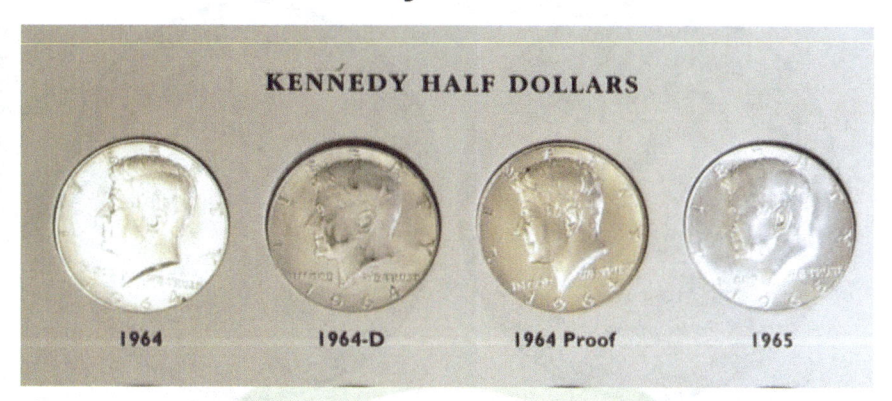

1964 | 1964-D | 1964 Proof | 1965

The Kennedy half dollar will have mint marks on the obverse and reverse of the coins depending on the date. There will be a no mint mark as well as a P, D, or S mint mark for these coins. Here are some examples.

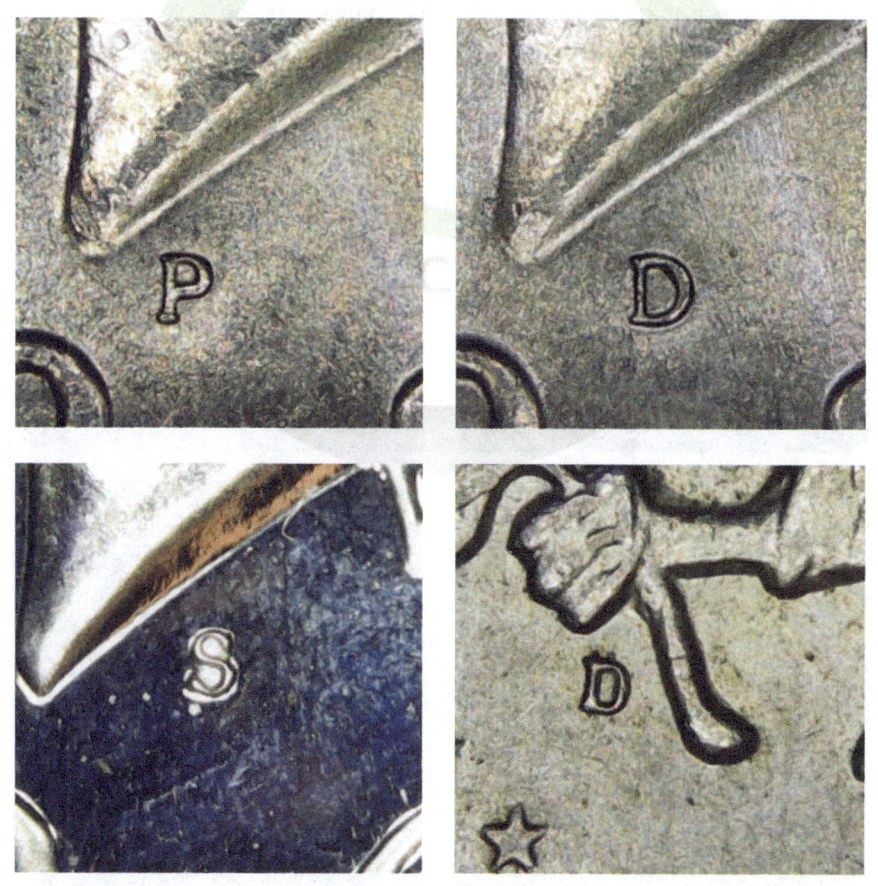

68

Mint Marks
Seated Liberty Dollar

Image courtesy of Professional Coin Grading Service (pcgs.com)

The silver Seated Liberty one dollar coin will either have no mint mark, an "S", "O" or "CC" mint mark on the reverse of the coin at the bottom under the eagle.

Mint Marks

Peace Dollar

Image courtesy of Professional Coin Grading Service (pcgs.com)

The silver Peace dollar coin will either have no mint mark, a "D" or "S" mint mark on the reverse of the coin under the word "ONE". These mint marks are very small and difficult to see with the naked eye.

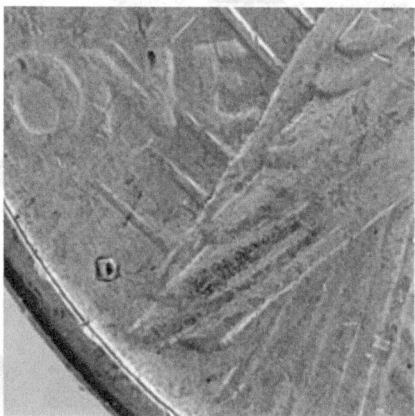

Mint Marks
Morgan Dollar

Image: Justin Couch

You will find the mint marks for the silver Morgan dollars on the reverse of the coin at the bottom. There will be dates with no mint marks at all, as well as an O, D, S, and CC mint mark. The 1921 D Morgan dollar was the only year that the Morgan dollar used the D mint mark.

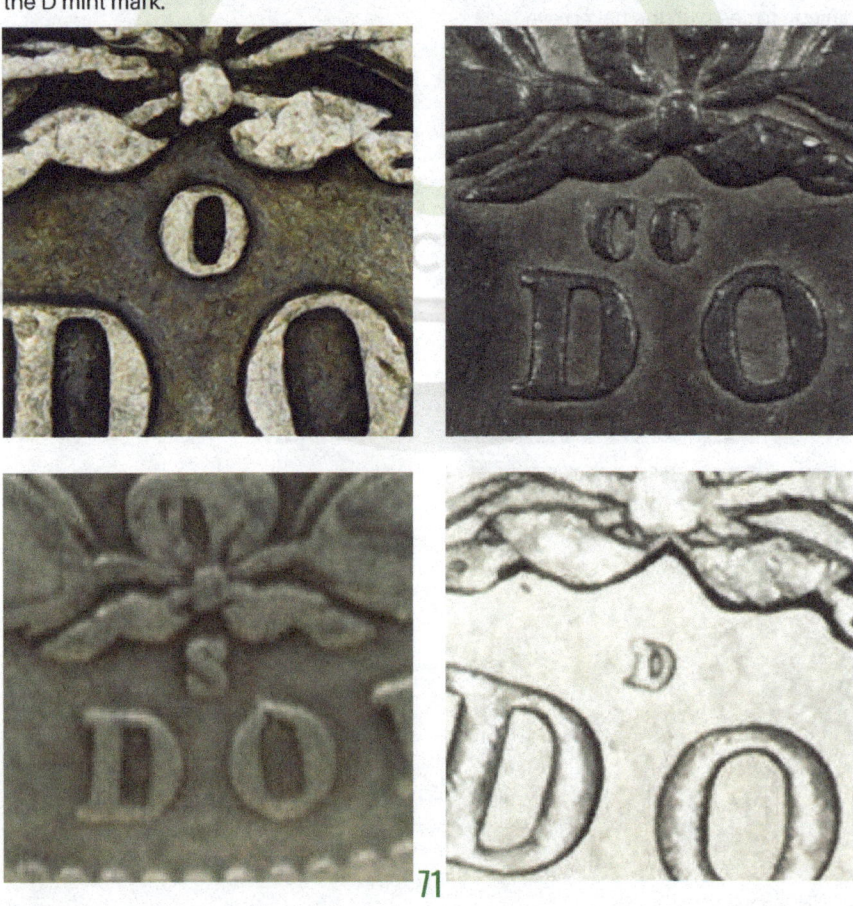

Mint Marks
Eisenhower Dollar

1971   1971-D   1971-S Silver Clad

The Eisenhower dollar also known as the "IKE" dollar coin will have either no mint mark at all, a "D" mint mark, or an "S" mint mark on the obverse of the coin.

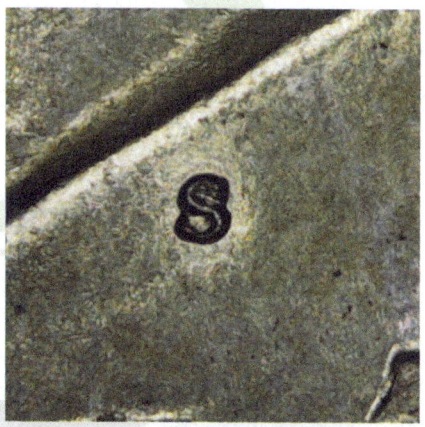

1971-S Silver Clad Proof   1972   1972-D

Mint Marks
Susan B. Anthony Dollar

You will find the mint mark for the Susan B. Anthony dollar coin on the obverse of the coin. There will be a P, D, or S mint mark.

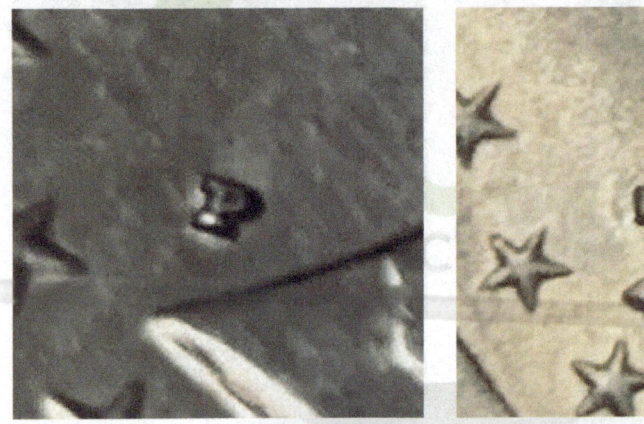

73

Mint Marks
List of Missing Mint Mark Coins

Some coins are not suppose to have a mint mark at all, however there are coins that were suppose to have a mint mark but are missing their mint mark. Here is a listing of coins to look for with missing mint marks. The proof coins you will have to look for in proof sets. If you know people selling proof sets, always look for these first two coins of the list.

Image courtesy of Professional Coin Grading Service (pcgs.com)

- 1975 Proof No "S" Roosevelt Dime
- 1990 Proof No "S" Lincoln Cent
- 1982 No "P" Roosevelt Dime
- 1922 No "D" Lincoln Cent Wheat Reverse

1975 D JEFFERSON NICKEL MISPLACED MINT MARK

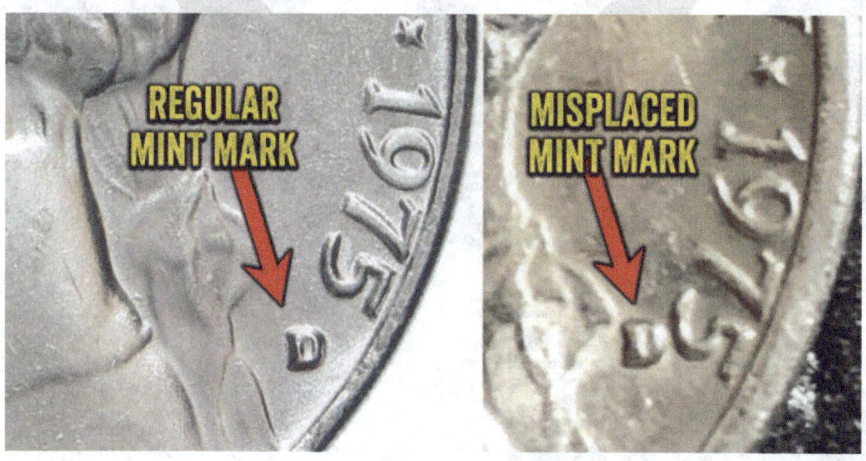

Always be on the look out for this rare misplaced "D" mint mark on the 1975 D Jefferson nickel. The coin on the right sold on eBay for $500.00

COIN COLLECTING SUPPLIES

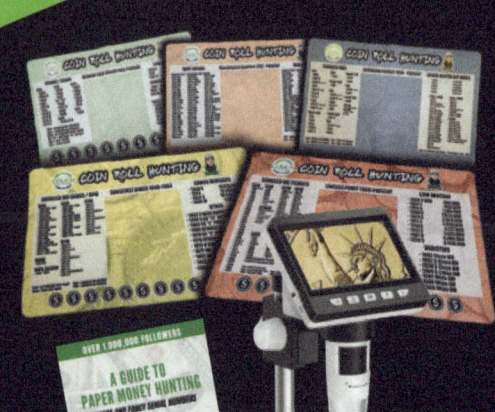

COUCH COLLECTIBLES

DEALS

COIN MICROSCOPES
COIN LOUPES
SILVER COINS
COIN MATS
COIN HUNTING CARDS
COIN SCALES
AND SO MUCH MORE!

WWW.COUCHCOLLECTIBLES.COM

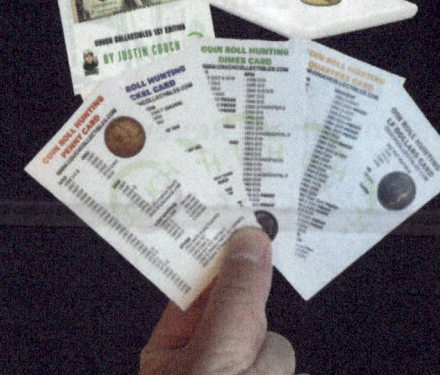

SCAN ME

SCAN ME FOR DEALS

Wide AM vs Close AM

Some coins are suppose to have wide "AM's" on "America" on the reverse of the Lincoln cent. Others are suppose to have close "AM's". Here is a list of coins you should look for that does not have the correct "AM" on the reverse of the Lincoln penny. In the images below you will also see a 1988 Wide AM Lincoln cent. ***Images: Justin Couch***

1. 1988 Wide AM (With the reverse of the 1989. Look for the FG initals where the "G" goes inward and drops below the lower curve, not the straight line "G".)
2. 1988 D Wide AM (Same as the 1988 no mint mark)
3. 1992 Close AM - Extremely Rare
4. 1992 D Close AM
5. 1996 Wide AM
6. 1998 S Close AM Proof
7. 1999 S Close AM Proof
8. 1999 Wide AM
9. 1998 Wide AM
10. 2000 Wide AM - Least Rare

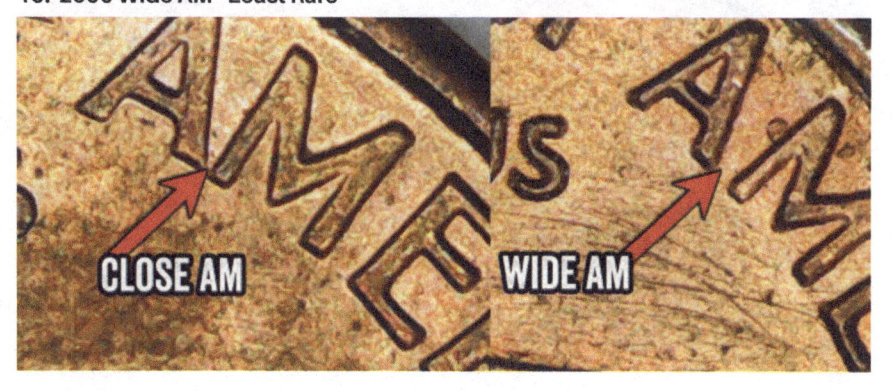

Error and Varieties

Mint-made errors are essentially mistakes on a coin made by the U.S. mint during the minting process. Groups of coins with distinctive characteristics are known as varieties. The term variety applies to coins with both intended and unintended differences while the term error refers only to coins with unintended differences.

Blank Planchet

The above image shows each blank planchet for the Washington quarter, Jefferson nickel, Lincoln penny and Roosevelt dime in comparison to the final result of each coin after they have been struck. The *Image: Justin Couch*

The image above shows numerous one cent blank planchets before the Lincoln cent design is struck onto them to create the coin. *Image: Justin Couch*

Error and Varieties

Broadstrike

The images above show a Jefferson nickel coin and a Lincoln wheat cent that has been broadstuck. ***Images: Justin Couch***

Broadstrike

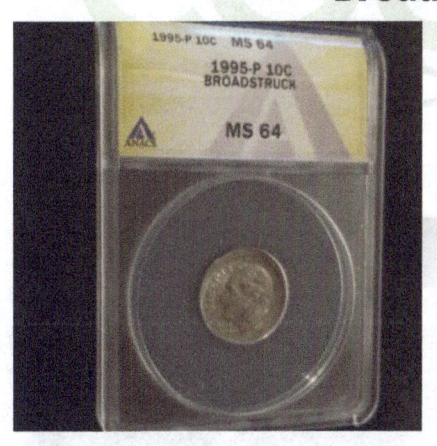

A broad strike is a coin that is struck outside the collar. The above images is a coin from Couch Collectibles coin collection. This is a 1995 Roosevelt dime that has been broad struck. ***Images: Justin Couch***

Error and Varieties
Broadstrike

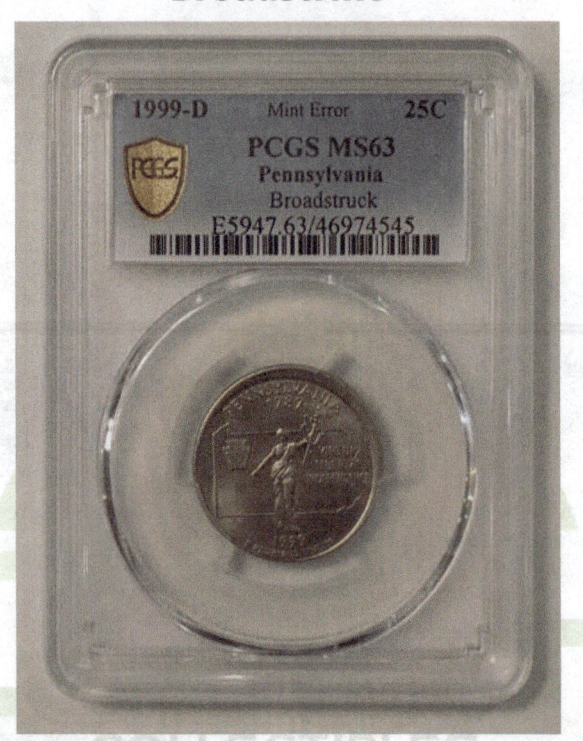

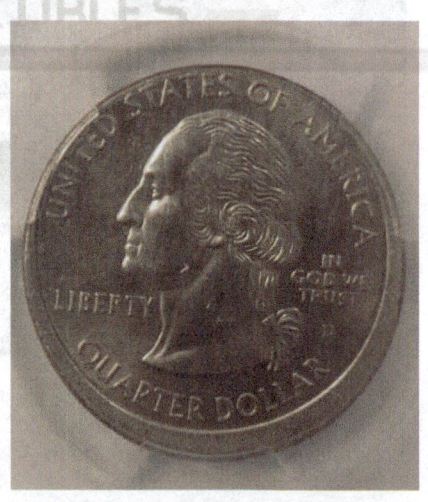

You can search for broadstrike errors on older and modern coins. As you see in the images above, a broadstrike mint error has taken place on a state quarter from 1999.
Images: Justin Couch

Error and Varieties
Broadstrike/Brockage

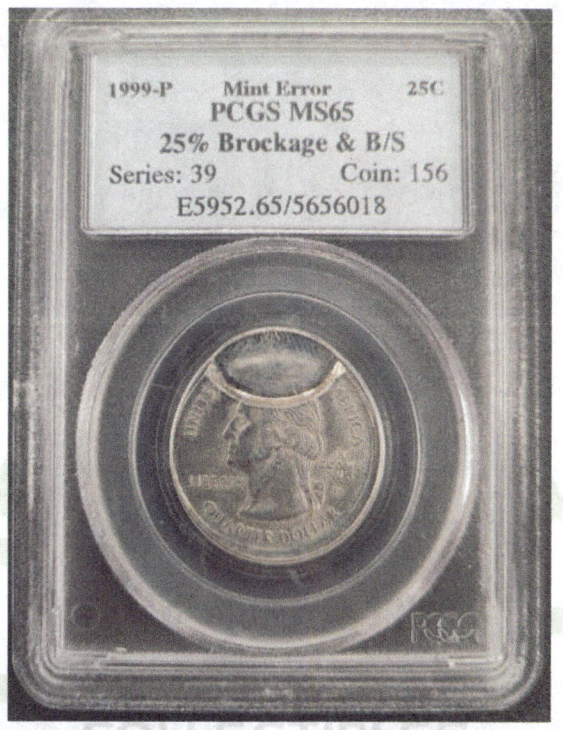

This is an extreme type of mint error that not only has a broadstrike error but also a brockage error. *Images: Justin Couch*

Error and Varieties
Brockage

A brockage error is a type of mint error coin where one side of the coin has the normal design and the opposite side has a mirror image of the same design impressed upon it. In the above image you will see this no dated Lincoln cent has a brockage and indent error. *Image: Chuck9999 eBay Seller*

Clipped Planchet

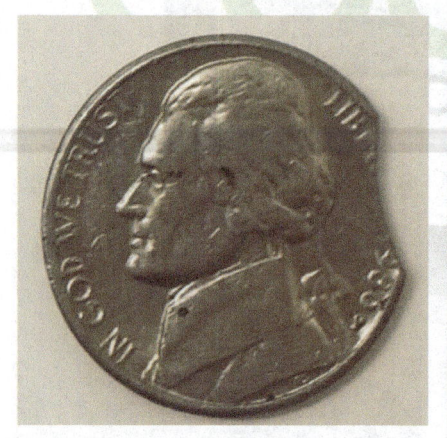

Here on the left is a 1986 D Jefferson nickel with a clip error from Couch Collectibles coin collection. The picture on the right is a Lincoln wheat cent with a clipped planchet found by Justin Couch in a coin collection. You can look for these mint errors on other denominations of coins as well. *Images: Justin Couch*

81

Error and Varieties
Cracked Planchet

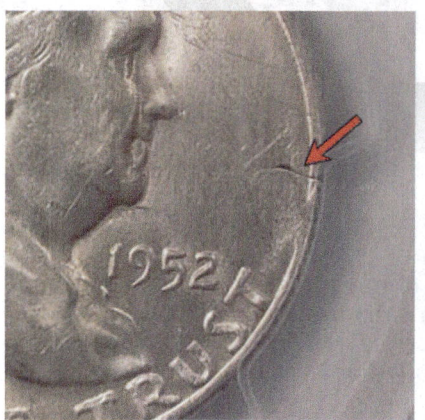

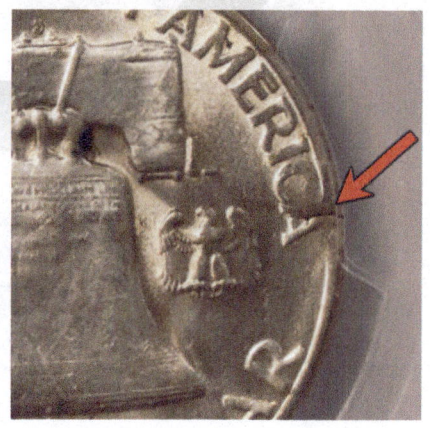

A cracked planchet can occur on just about any type of coin. This will add some value to the coin however the price depends on which coin you have with cracked planchet, the size of the crack and of course the grade of the coin. *Images: Justin Couch*

Error and Varieties
Counter Brockage

Counter brockages are created when a capped die strikes a coin that has already been struck, and the obverse design is impressed into the cap. This will result in a design where the cap face will be an incuse brockage. *Image: Chuck9999 eBay Seller*

Die Break (Cud)

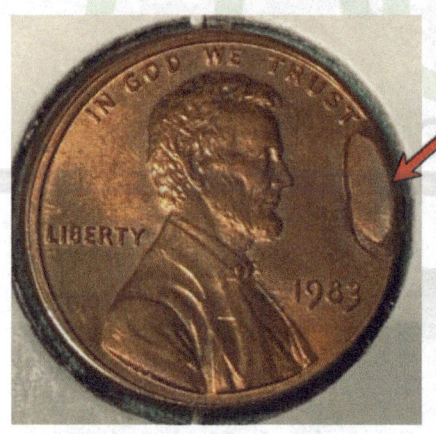

You will see the large cud on the right side of this Lincoln cent. These are coins that are struck after the break falls away, have a raised, rounded, and unstruck area along the edge. These are known as cuds. They can be small or large. The larger cud's in most cases are more desirable to collectors. *Image: Bryan Hooper, Tricia Musi*

Error and Varieties
Die Break & Die Chips

On the 2008 Arizona state quarter you want to look for what is known as the "extra cactus". This is a result of a die break where the initials on the coin is covered. Below you will see images of the differences. These coins sell between $3 - $5 on eBay however extremely high graded examples could sell for much more. *Images: Justin Couch*

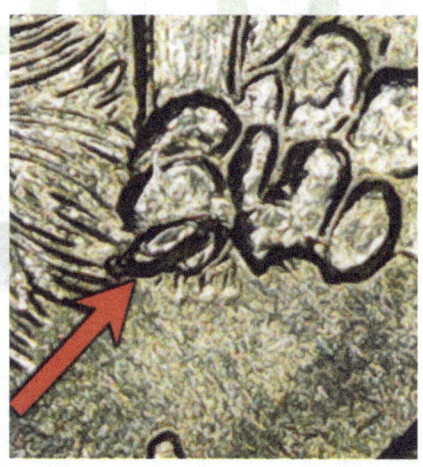

The left image depicts a regular Arizona state quarter where you can see the full initials on the reverse of the coin. The right image will show you the extra cactus that partially covers the initials.

84

Error and Varieties
Die Break & Die Chips

You will see an interior die break on this 2020 Lincoln cent taking place on Lincoln's head. This can add extra value to your coin as coin collectors are willing to pay more than face value to add them to their coin collections.
Images: Justin Couch

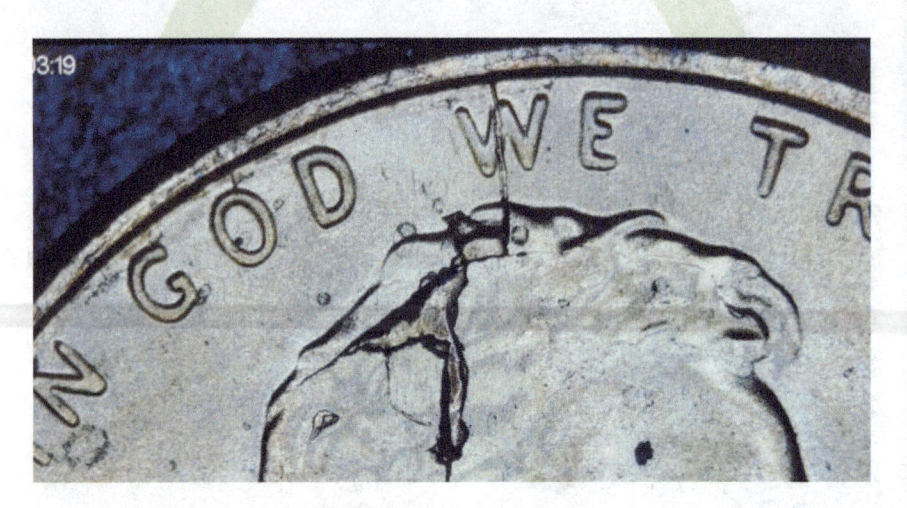

Error and Varieties
Die Break & Die Chips

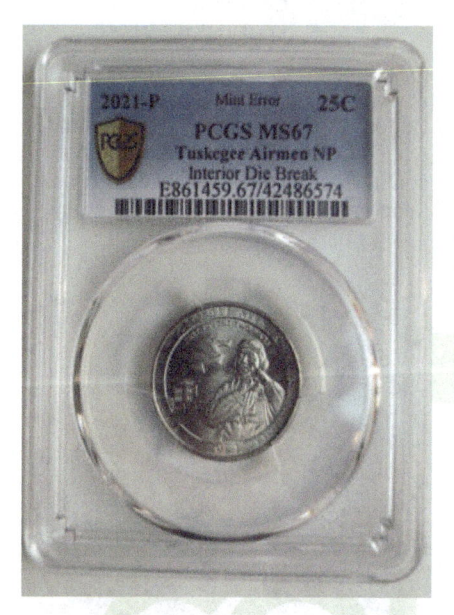

On the 2021 Tuskgee Airman quarter you can look for a small die break on the wing of the airplane. This interior die break adds some extra value to the quarter.

Typically when new mint error coins are discovered they sell very well on the secondary market when they are found early in the year.

Once more collectors discover the same error, the values tend to decrease as more become available to market.

Images: Justin Couch

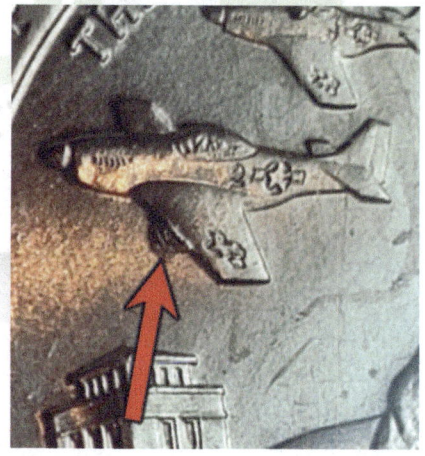

Error and Varieties
Die Break & Die Chips

Carlos Perez who is a paid member of Couch Collectibles YouTube channel sent the image on the left of a die break taking place on a 1980's Lincoln cent.

Image: Carlos Perez

Image: Micahel M.

The image above shows a very large die break on a 1991 Lincoln Cent. Typically the larger the die break, the more valuable these mint errors will be on the secondary market. Nice find Michael!

Error and Varieties
Die Break & Die Chips

Image: Justin Couch

The 2022 Wilma Mankiller quarter has been a hot modern coin to search for in coin rolls from the bank. You want to look for a die break on these quarters as that mint error has added a great deal of value to these coins.

Examples of these mint error quarters have been selling on the secondary market for hundreds of dollars. The grade of the coin and the stage of the mint error will determine what a collector is willing to pay for these quarters.

Error and Varieties
Die Break & Die Chips

The image to the left is a small die break taking place on a 2005 state quarter. Typically smaller die breaks like these will be lower end mint error coins depending on the coin grade.

Image: Justin Couch

Image: Justin Couch

The image above shows a very large die break on the top of George Washington's hat. This is a modern 2021 quarter many collectors are searching for in circulation.

Image: Rodney S.

The image above shows a die break on a Washington Quarter.

Image: Amanda Deines

The image above shows a small die chip on the right side of the Monticello building of the Jefferson nickel reverse.

Error and Varieties
Die Break & Die Chips

Here are two different examples of die chips resulting in a digit of the dates to be filled. A die chip can be connected to a die crack or it can be freestanding. These coins are not super valuable but something I enjoy finding when coin roll hunting.
Images: Justin Couch

The die chip taking place in the above image on the word liberty is often referred to as the "BIE Penny" because of the placement of the die chip. You can search for these when you are coin roll hunting with a USB coin microscope available on https://www.couchcollectibles.com.

Error and Varieties
Die Break & Die Chips

While your coin roll hunting, look for die chips on the reverse of the 2024 quarter featuring Dr. Mary Edwards Walker. *Images: Justin Couch*

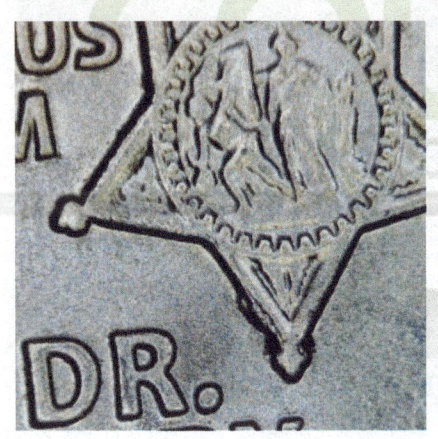

You can spot the die chips on the star, the lettering and on the shoulder of Dr. Mary Edwards Walker. Search for these when you are coin roll hunting with a USB coin microscope available on https://www.solo.to/couchcollectibles

Error and Varieties
Die Break & Die Chips

Here is an example of a small die chip at the bottom of the 2015 Homestead quarter. This quarter is referred to by collectors as the "Leaky Bucket" quarter. ***Images: Justin Couch***

Error and Varieties
Die Break & Die Chips

Look for a small die chip on Washington's nose on the 2024 quarter. ***Images: Justin Couch***

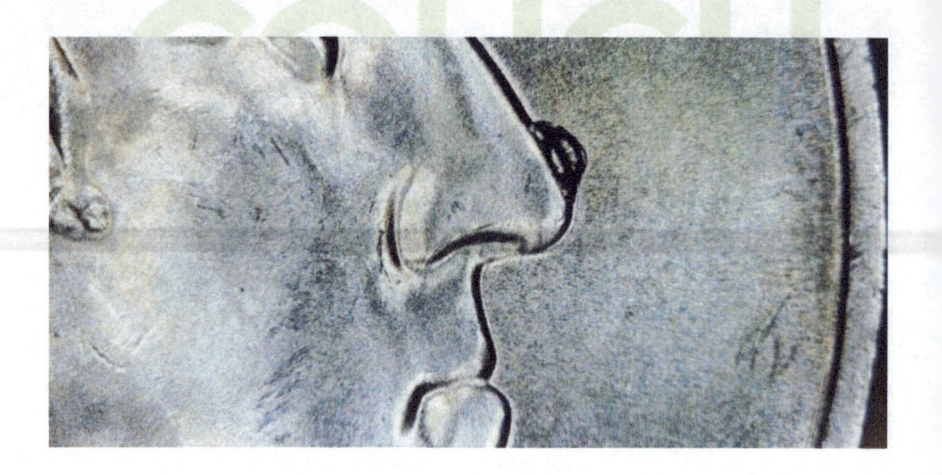

Error and Varieties
Die Cap

I found this die cap 1982 Lincoln penny in a coin roll from the bank. Believe it or not, I also found an Indian head penny in the same roll! I'm sure that will never happen again. *Images: Justin Couch*

Here is the true view image of my coin from PCGS (Professional Coin Grading Service). You can select true view on your coin grading submission form for an extra $10.00.

Error and Varieties
Die Clash

A die clash coin is a mint error coin that occurs when two coin dies come together without a coin between them. Here is a 1984 Lincoln cent with a die clash. You will notice the pillars from the Lincoln memorial reverse on the obverse of the coin.

You'll also see a die clash error taking place on the 2021 Lincoln Cent in the image below. The lines from the shield on the reverse of the coin appear on the obverse as a result.

Images: Justin Couch

Error and Varieties
Die Clash

Images: Shelia G.

These images of the 2021 Jefferson Nickel show an amazing die clash error discovered by Shelia G. a subscriber and paid member of Couch Collectibles YouTube channel. Nice find Shelia!

Images: Shelia G.

Error and Varieties
Die Clash

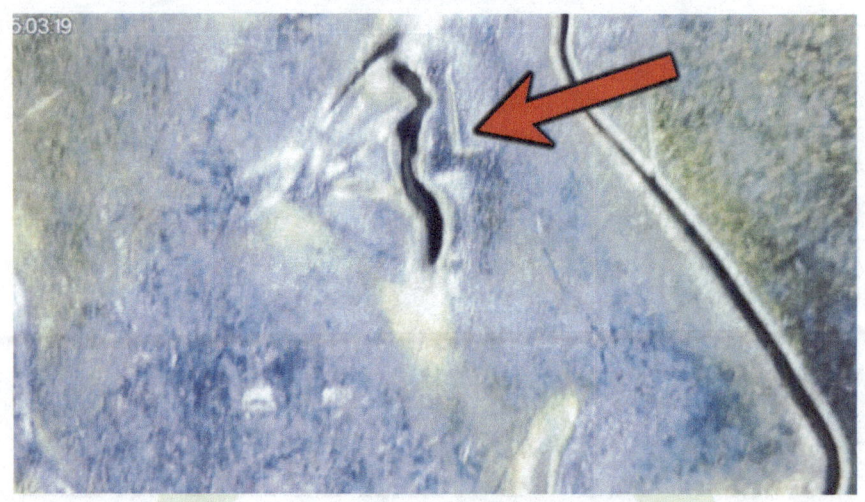

Image: Justin Couch

Check your 2024 quarters for a die clash with the "HOPE" reverse. You can see the reverse lettering coming through on the obverse of the coin to the right of Washington's eye.

You will need a coin microscope or coin loupe to see this die clash. You can get those items and other coin supplies at https://www.solo.to/couchcollectibles

Images: Justin Couch

97

Error and Varieties
Die Clash

Images: Justin Couch

These images of a 2024 Quarter dollar show a small die clash on the obverse of the coin to the right and left of Washington's pony tail.

Error and Varieties
Die Clash

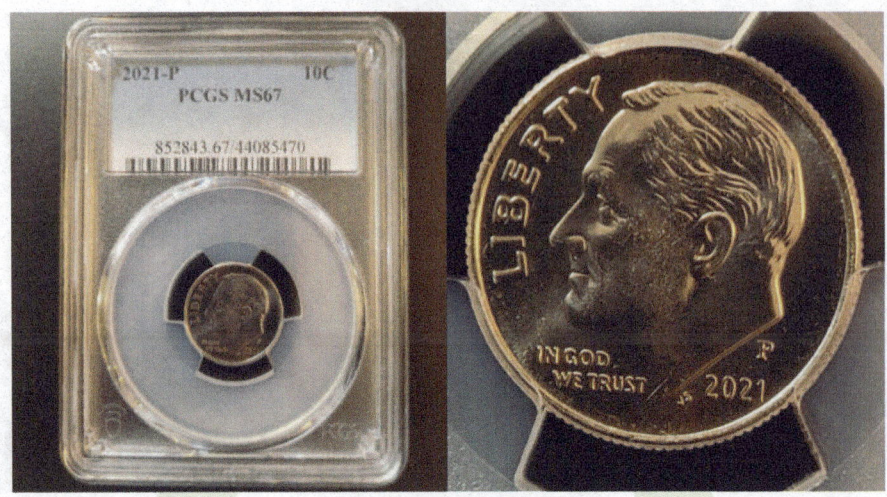

Images: Justin Couch

These image below shows a close up example of a die clash on the obverse of a 2021 Roosevelt dime. You will need a coin microscope or coin loupe to see this example. Coin collecting supplies is available at https://www.solo.to/couchcollectibles

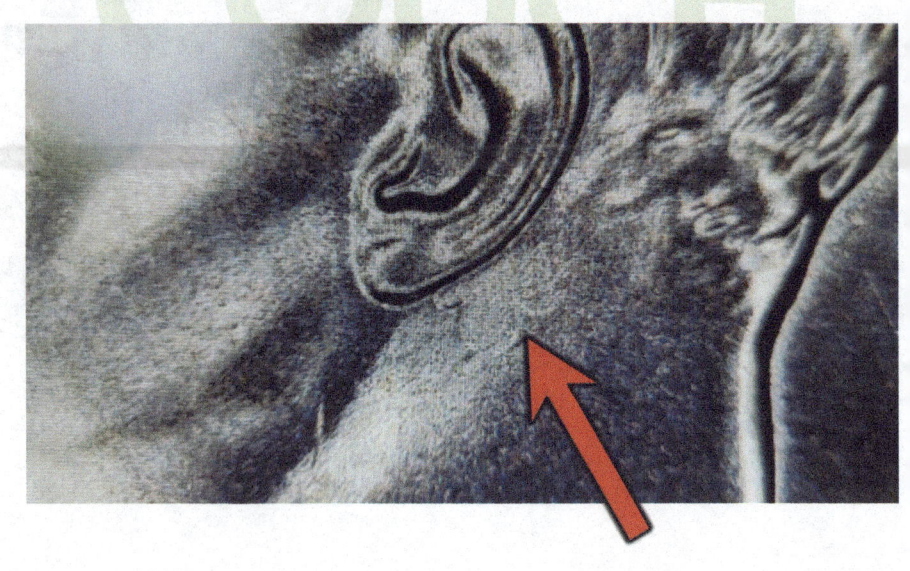

Error and Varieties
Die Clash

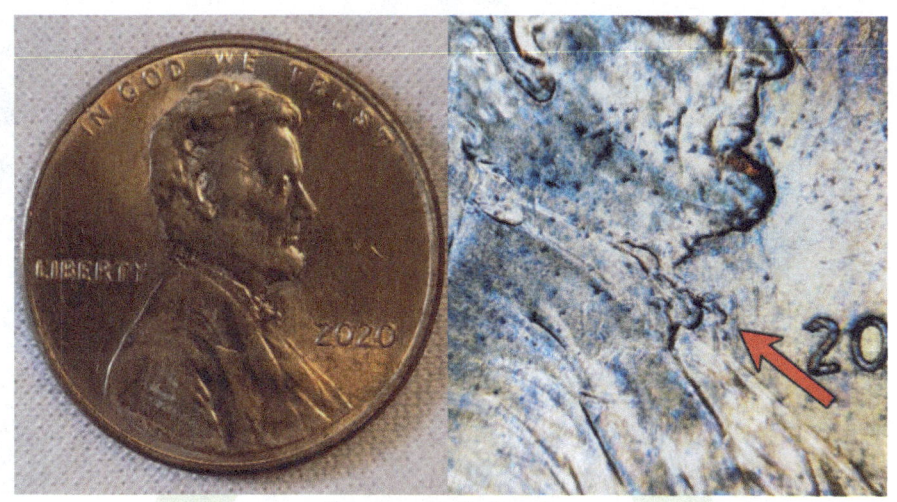

Images: Justin Couch

These image below shows a close up example of a die clash on the obverse of a 2020 Lincoln shield cent. You may need a coin microscope or coin loupe to see the "E. Pluribus Unum lettering from the reverse coming through on the obverse. Coin collecting supplies is available at https://www.solo.to/couchcollectibles

Error and Varieties
Die Clash

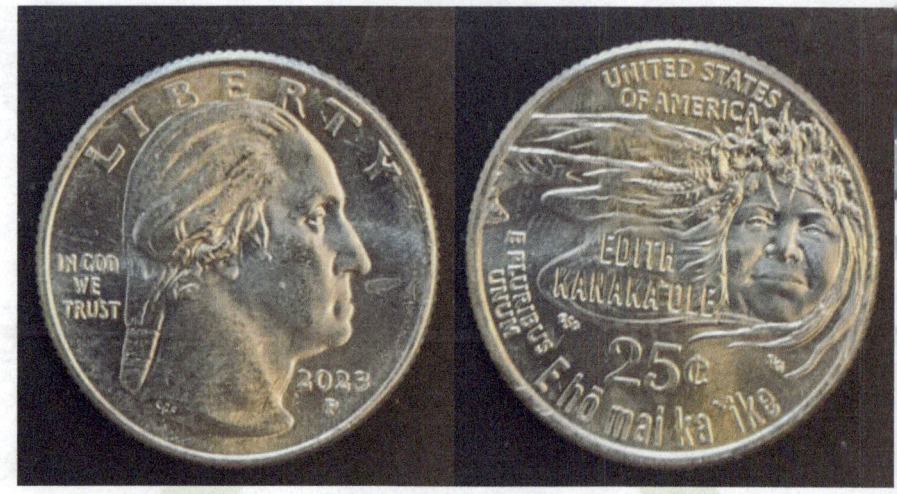

Images: Justin Couch

Look for this amazing die clash on your 2023 quarters. You will see the name "EDITH" from the reverse design showing on the obverse of the coin by Washington's ear and in his hair. This has been a hot coin to find in the last couple years as the die clash adds value to the coin. Coin collecting supplies is available at https://www.solo.to/couchcollectibles

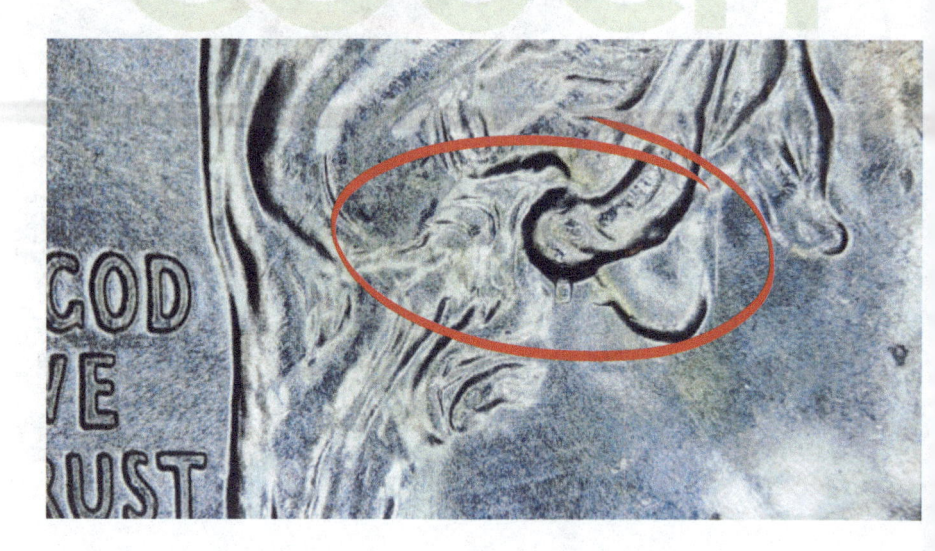

Error and Varieties
Die Crack

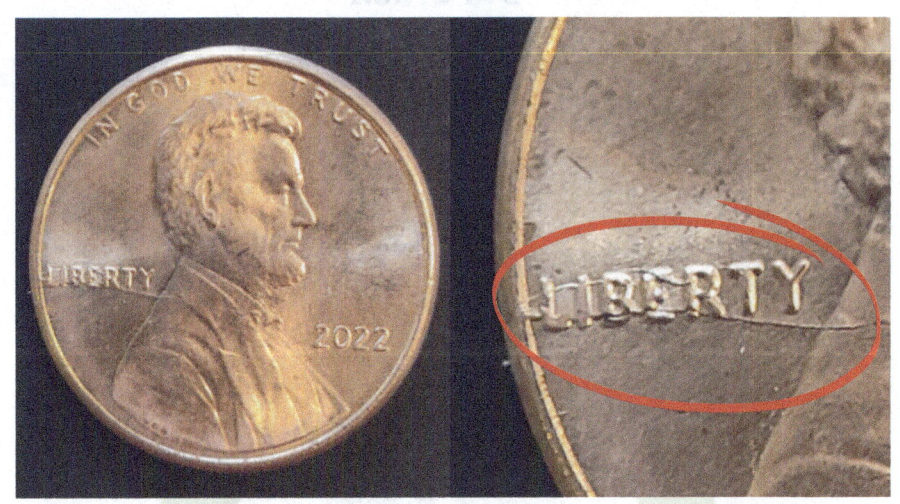

Images: Justin Couch

You can search for die cracks on just about any type of coinage. The images above features a die crack on a 2022 P Lincoln cent's obverse, while the bottom images show a die crack on the reverse of a 2022 D Lincoln cent. These are not super valuable coins but some collectors will pay a few dollars a piece for them. Coin collecting supplies is available at https://www.solo.to/couchcollectibles

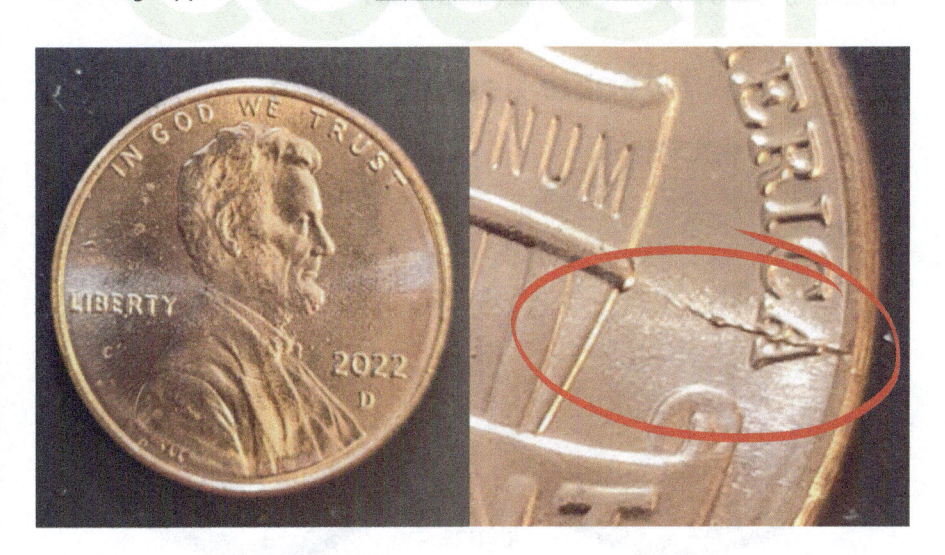

Error and Varieties
Die Crack

Here is an example of a die crack on the 1999 Delaware state quarter. You can see the die crack coming from the mouth of the horse on the reverse of the coin. This is often referred to as the "Spitting Horse" quarter. You can look for die cracks on all other denominations of coins. ***Images: Justin Couch***

Double Denomination

A double denomination is when a coin is struck a second time by dies from a different denomination. In the above image you will see the Lincoln cent and Roosevelt dime designs on the coin as a result of the mint error. ***Image courtesy of Professional Coin Grading Service (pcgs.com)***

Error and Varieties
Die Gouge

Here is an example of a die gouge on a 2020 Quarter. A die gouge is when a foreign object is dragged across, and digs into, the die face. This will result in raised areas on the coin's surface. *Images: Justin Couch*

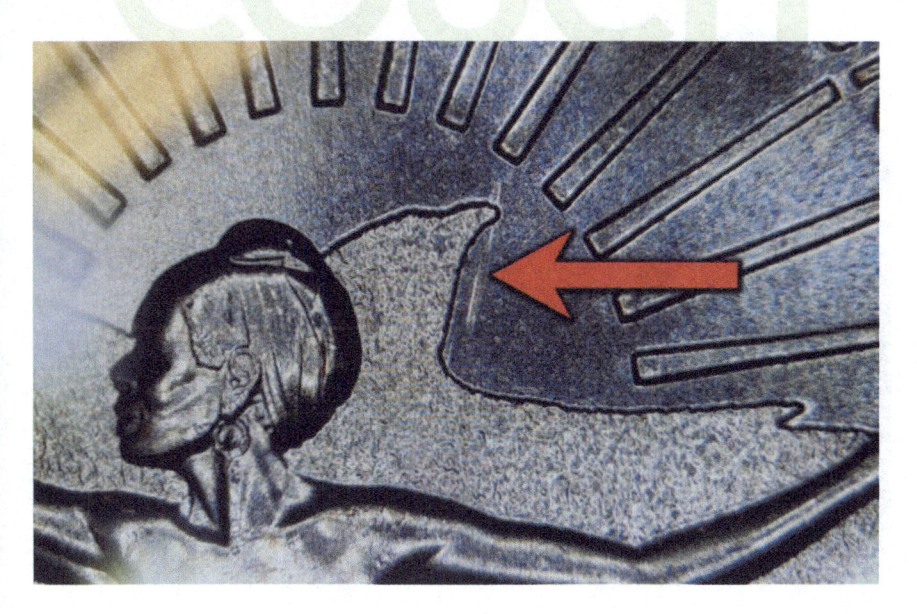

Error and Varieties
Detached Leg

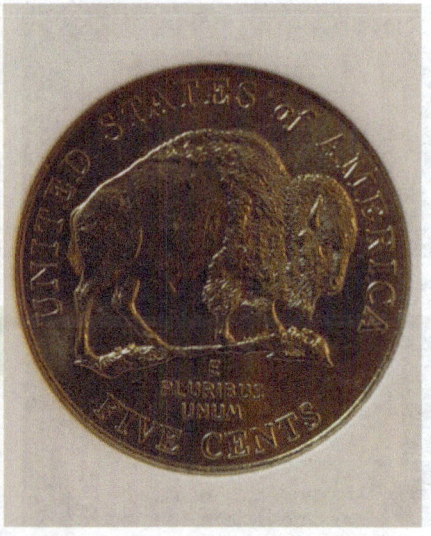

Here is an example of a detached leg on a 2005 Jefferson nickel. This is something you can look for in coin rolls from the bank or in your coin jars that can add value to your nickel. *Images: Justin Couch*

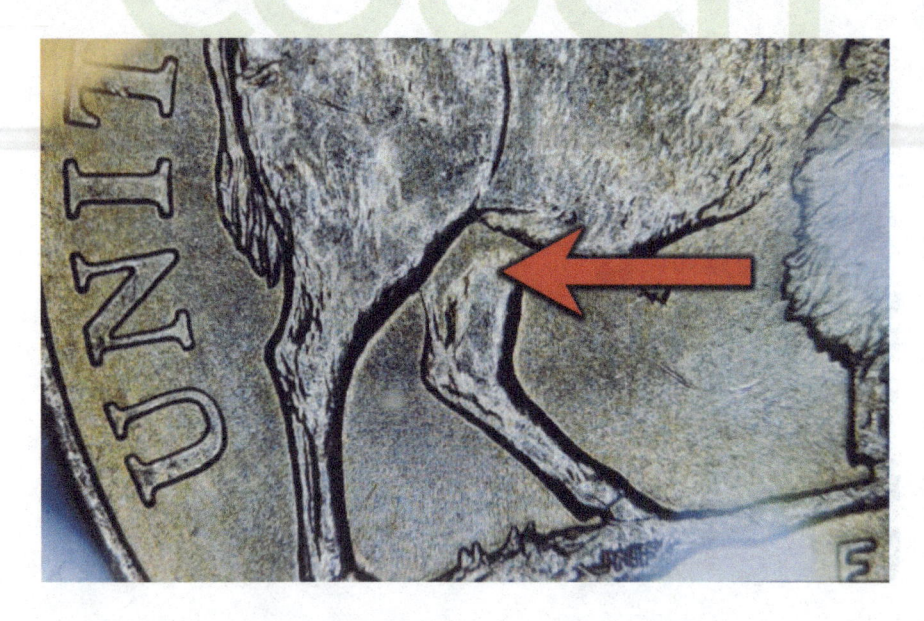

Error and Varieties
Doubled Die

You can look for a 2019 doubled die obverse Lincoln cent in coin rolls from the bank or even in your pocket change. Look for extra thickness on the date of the coin.
Image: Justin Couch

Doubled Die

This 2014 Lincoln cent with a doubled die obverse was found coin roll hunting by Jeff Chapman, a long time subscriber of Couch Collectibles YouTube channel. If you would like for me to review pictures of your coins, press the blue join button on my YouTube channel and become a level 2 member. *Image: Jeff Chapman*

Error and Varieties
Doubled Die

A new hot modern coin that collectors are searching for is the 2023 Kennedy half dollar coin with a doubled die obverse. Look for doubling on the lettering and the date. *Images: Justin Couch*

Error and Varieties
Doubled Dies

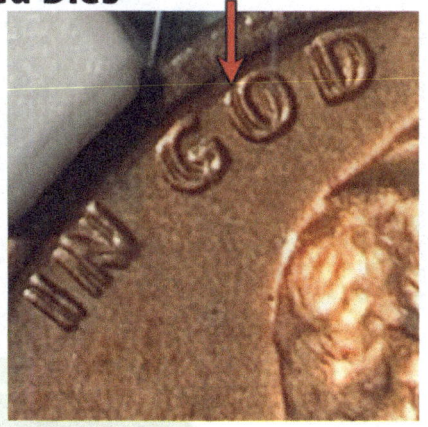

A doubled die occurs when a die receives an additional, misaligned impression from the hub. You can search for these on various different coins. I will have a list later in this book about which dates to look for. This is a 1972 doubled die obverse Lincoln cent. ***Images: Bryan Hooper***

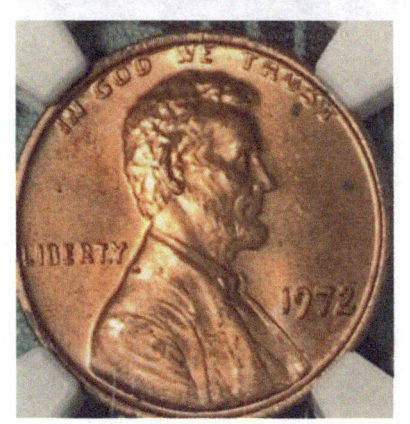

This is one of my favorite mint error coins. You can easily find 1972 Lincoln cents in a bank roll, however finding a doubled die error is the difficult part. Don't give up!

Be sure to subscribe to Bryan Hooper on YouTube for videos of his amazing coin collection.

108

Error and Varieties
Doubled Dies

Look for doubling on the obverse of the 2004 Jefferson nickel with the Handshake reverse. Doubling can occur on the lettering "In God We Trust", "Liberty" and "FS".
Images: Justin Couch

109

Error and Varieties
Doubled Dies

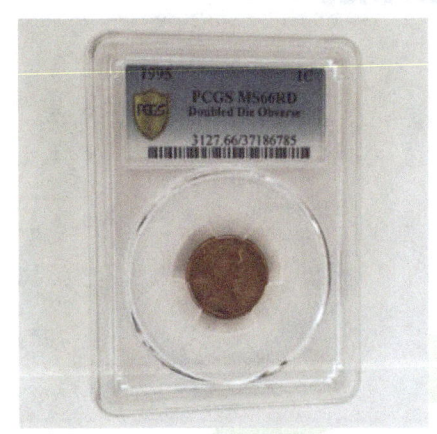

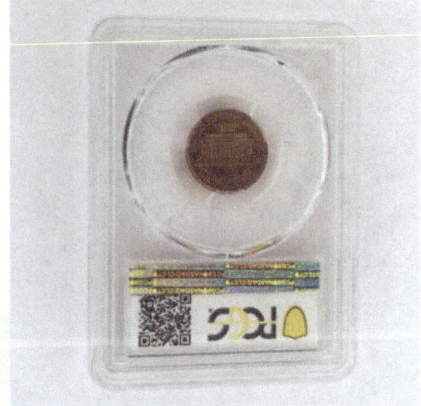

Here is an example of a 1995 Lincoln cent with a doubled die obverse. This is from Couch Collectibles's coin collection. *Images: Justin Couch*

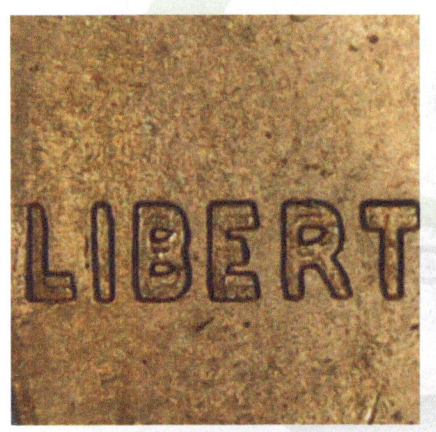

Error and Varieties
Doubled Dies

This is a 1934 Washington quarter with a doubled die obverse. You can look for doubling on the motto "In God We Trust" as well as on the word "Liberty" and the date. *Images: Justin Couch*

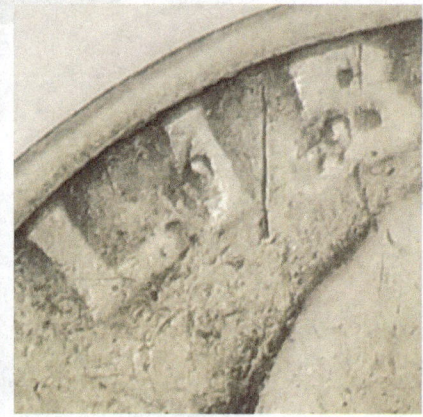

111

Error and Varieties
Doubled Dies

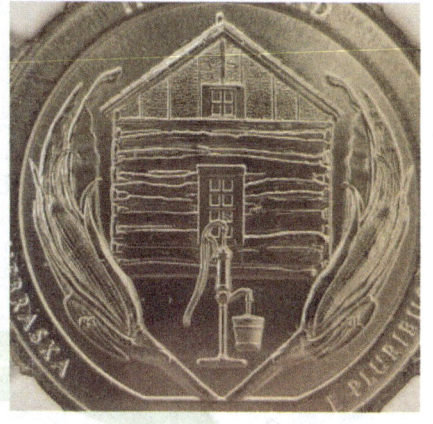

Here is a 2015 P doubled die reverse Homestead quarter. There are a variety of different doubled dies for this quarter however this is considered the "Best of" Variety by Wexler's coins. You can see the top of the water pump doubled in the window. You can also look for doubling on the windows of these coins. ***Images: Justin Couch***

Error and Varieties
Doubled Dies

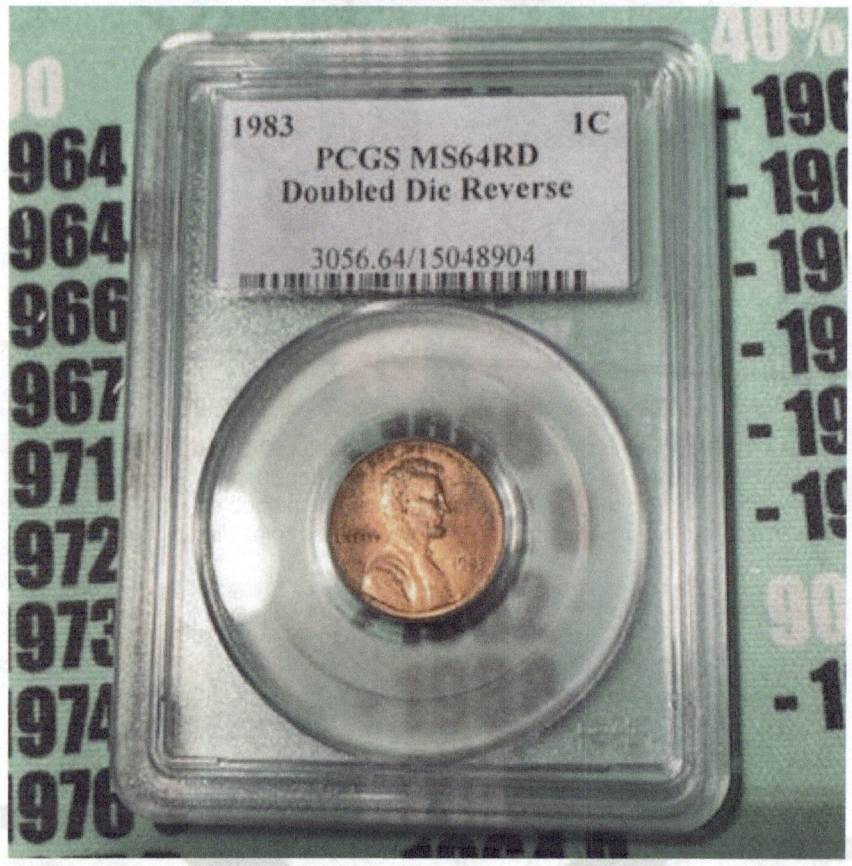

Here is an example of a 1983 doubled die reverse Lincoln cent. Again, you can look for different types of double dies on various different dates in which we have listed later in this book. *Images: Bryan Hooper*

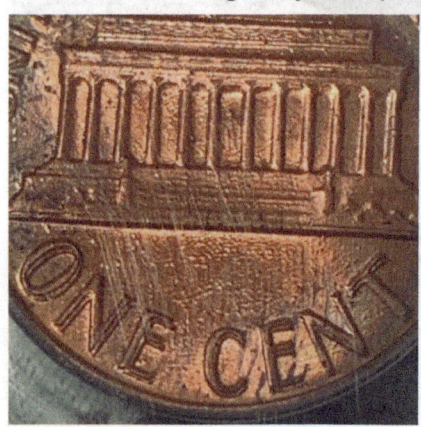

Error and Varieties
Doubled Dies

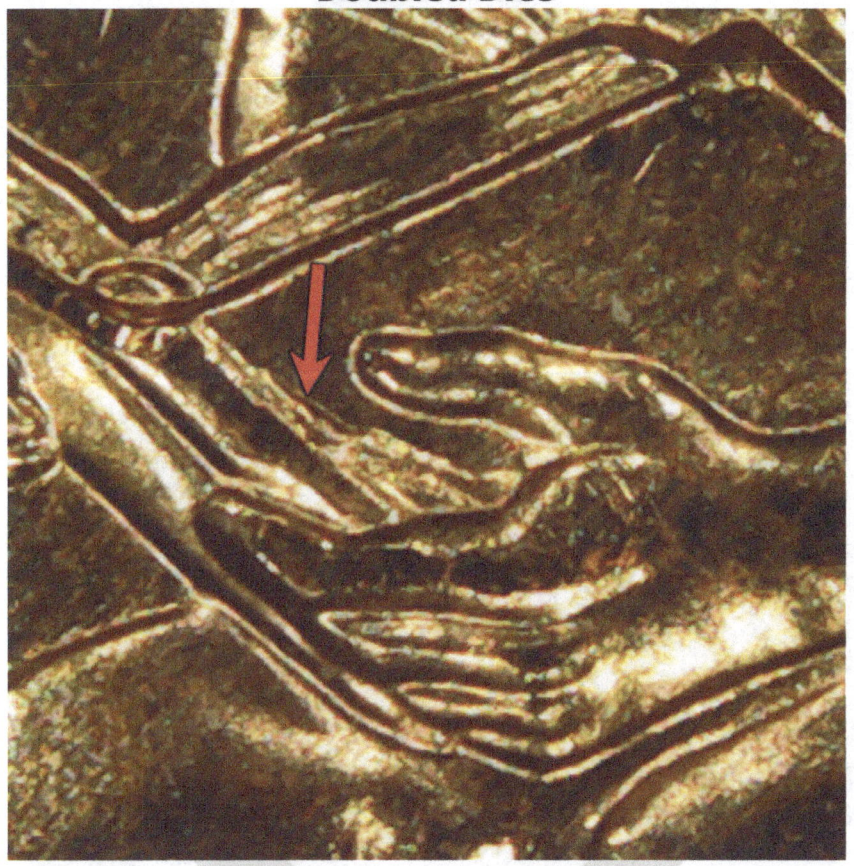

Here is an example of a 2009 doubled die reverse Lincoln cent. There are a wide variety of different DDR's for this penny. In the images you will notice doubling on Lincoln's finger. *Images: Justin Couch*

114

Error and Varieties
Doubled Dies

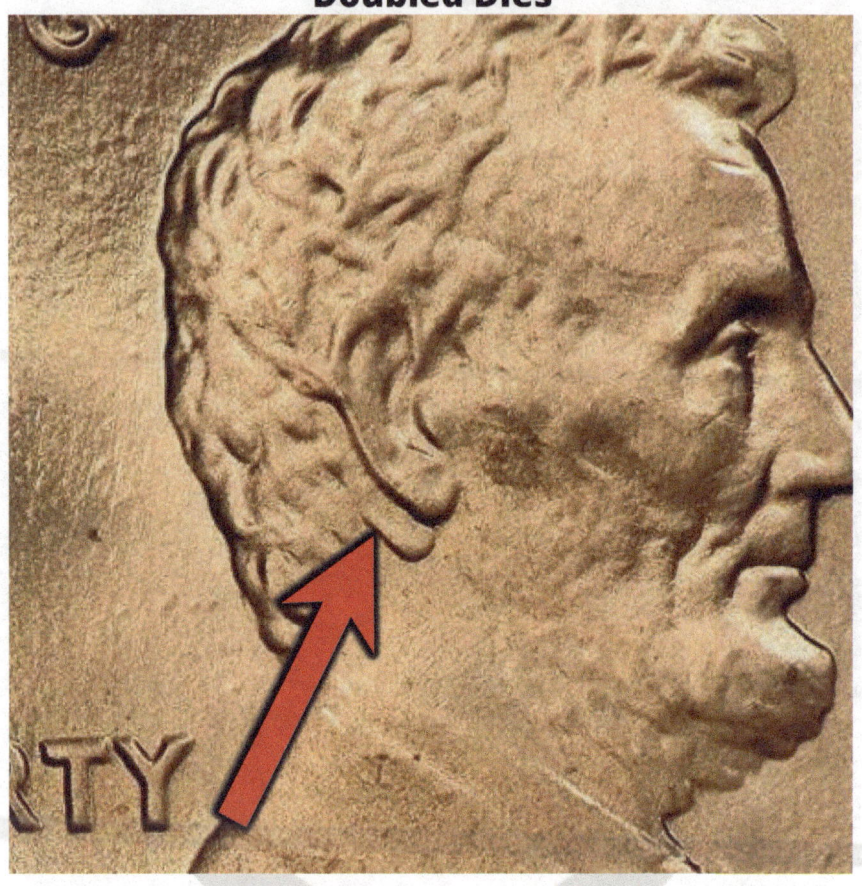

Here is an example of a 1984 doubled die obverse. Look for doubling on Lincoln's ear. *Image courtesy of Professional Coin Grading Service (pcgs.com)*

115

Error and Varieties
Double Strike

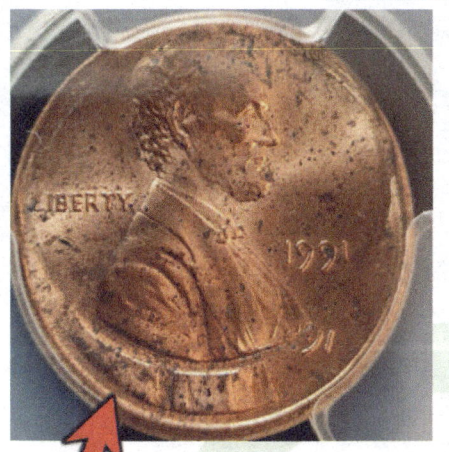

This is a double strike error on the 1991 Lincoln cent. This is an extremely rare mint error to find and can add a ton of value to your coin. ***Images: Justin Couch***

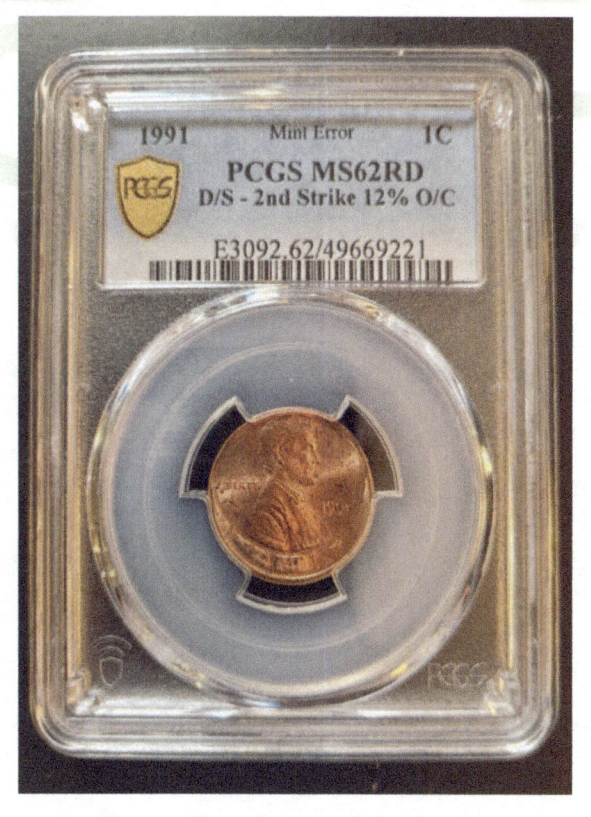

Error and Varieties
Double Strike

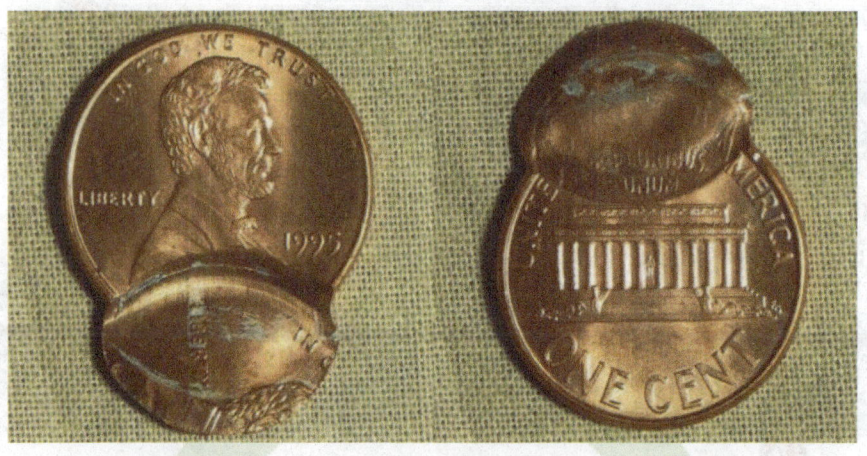

This is a double strike error on the 1995 Lincoln cent. A double strike is when a coin doesn't eject from the striking chamber properly and the die comes down to strike the coin a second time. *Image: Chuck9999 eBay Seller*

Double Strike

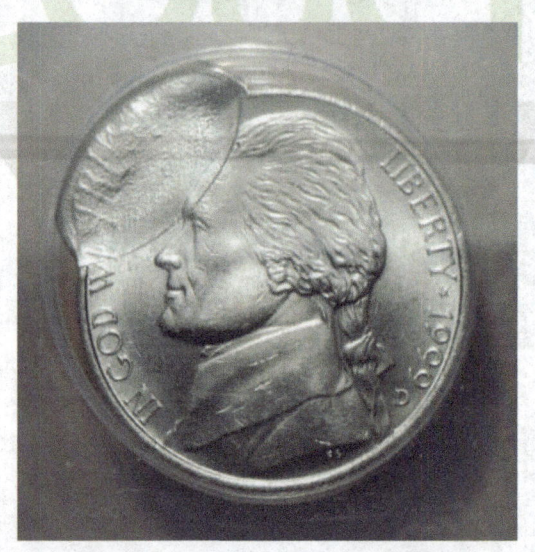

This 1999 Jefferson nickel has an extreme double strike. These types of coins are typically not found in bank rolls, rather in bank bags as they make their way through the riddler and out of the U.S. Mint to banks. *Image: Justin Couch*

Error and Varieties
Dropped Letter

Look for dropped letters on states quarters and even Lincoln pennies This dropped letter "R" is taking place on a 2007 D Utah state quarter. This can make your coin extremely valuable. *Images: Justin Couch*

118

Error and Varieties
Improperly Annealed Planchet

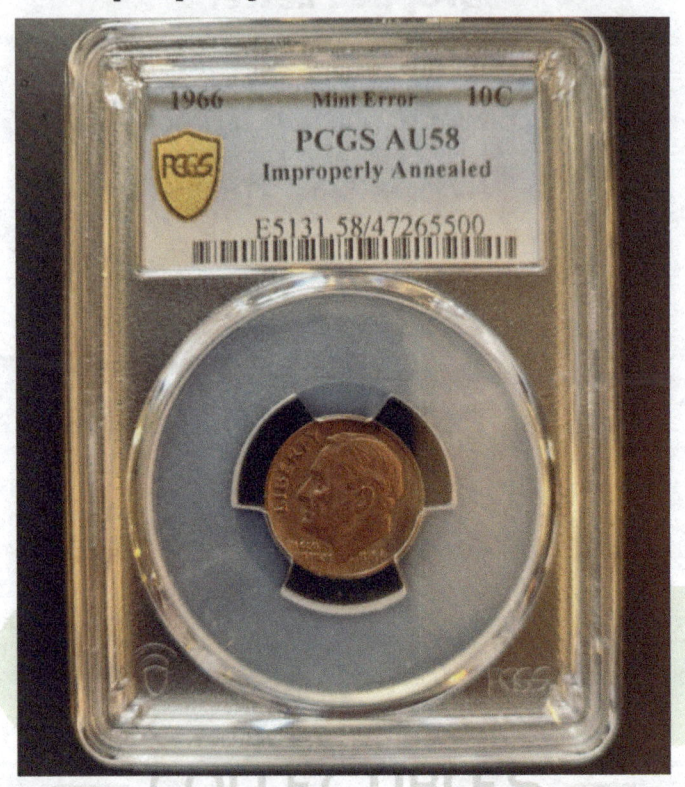

An Improperly Annealed Planchet is when the heat or cool mixture between striking's is off a bit, in which causes the coin being struck to have a colored appearance. ***Images: Justin Couch***

Error and Varieties

Indents

Here is a 1989 Lincoln cent with an indent error. This type of mint error is an indentation from an unstruck blank or planchet. *Images: Justin Couch*

Lamination

This is an Indian head cent with an obverse lamination error. Lamination errors are when the surface of a coin cracks and flakes. Be sure to follow ae_coins on Instagram for more amazing coin images. *Image: ae_coins Instagram*

Error and Varieties
Mated Pairs

Mated pairs are coins that are struck together and are usually separated during the sorting process. The above image displays mated pair Lincoln cents. ***Image: Chuck9999 eBay Seller.***

Missing Clad Layer

The above image is a 1968 Roosevelt dime that has a missing reverse clad layer. The outer clad layer is missing exposing the inner copper layer of the coin. ***Images: Justin Couch***

121

Error and Varieties
Missing Clad Layer

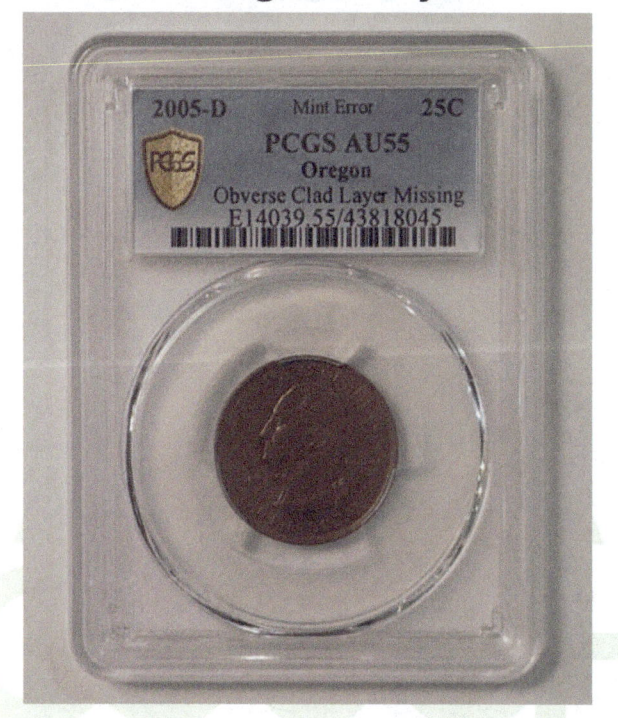

The above image is a 2005 state quarter that has a missing reverse clad layer. This type of mint error can happen on other denominations of coins also.
Images: Justin Couch

Error and Varieties
Missing Edge Lettering

These Presidential dollar coins are supposed to have the date and mint mark on the edge of the coin. If you find one that is missing the edge lettering, it can add value to your coin. ***Images: Justin Couch***

Error and Varieties
Muled Coins

The above image is one of the most famous muled coins. This is an example of a 2000 Sacagawea dollar muled with a quarter dollar. These types of coins can sell for tens of thousands of dollars. *Image courtesy of Professional Coin Grading Service (pcgs.com)*

1943 S Bronze Lincoln Wheat Cent

As we know in 1943 the Lincoln wheat cent was steel, not copper. In the above image you will see a super rare 1943 S bronze Lincoln wheat cent. There are many fake 1943 copper cents however genuine examples sell for hundreds of thousands of dollars. Check out the sold auctions on Heritage Auctions (www.HA.com) *Image courtesy of Professional Coin Grading Service (pcgs.com)*

Error and Varieties
Off Center

An off center error coin is produced when the coin is struck once off center. These coins can vary in value based on how far off center they are struck. Typically off center coins with full dates are more desirable by collectors than coins without a date or missing digits. *Images: Justin Couch*

Off Center

Here is an off center Roosevelt dime that I had graded by PCGS.

125

Error and Varieties
Off Center

Images: Daniel Hickman

This image was sent in by a paid member of Couch Collectibles YouTube Channel, Daniel Hickman.

Off Center

Images: Justin Couch

Some off center errors can be very common and affordable however others can be extremely valuable depending on the date of the coin, the percentage of the off center and the grade or condition of the coin.

Error and Varieties
Off Center

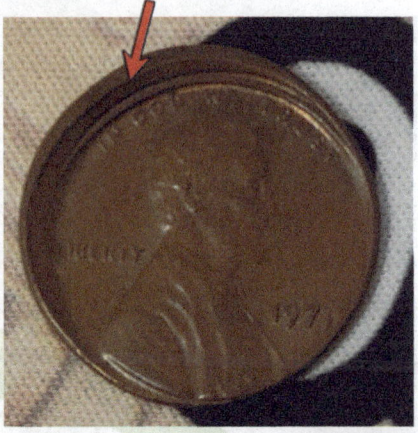

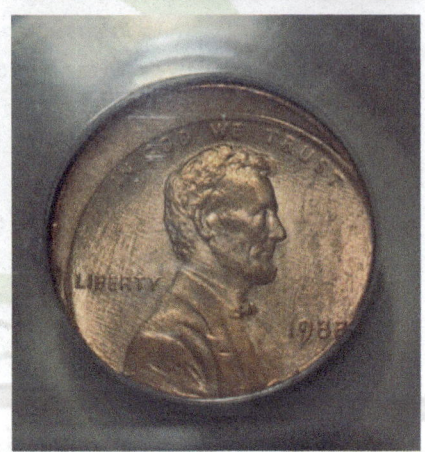

Images: Justin Couch

Error and Varieties
Partial Collar

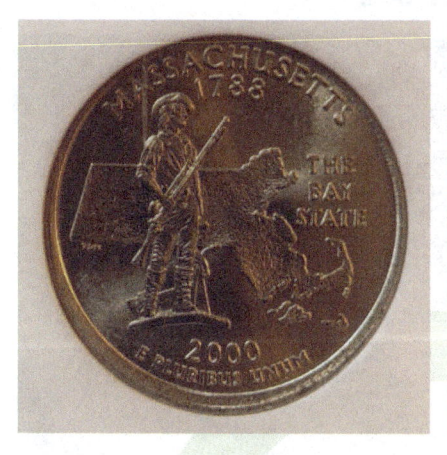

A partial collar occurs when there is a malfunction of the striking press. This results in the collar being in the wrong position. The lower die is then recessed in the collar. This allows the coin to have a formed rim. After a coin is struck, the lower die raises up, pushing the struck coin out of the collar and ejecting it. ***Images: Justin Couch***

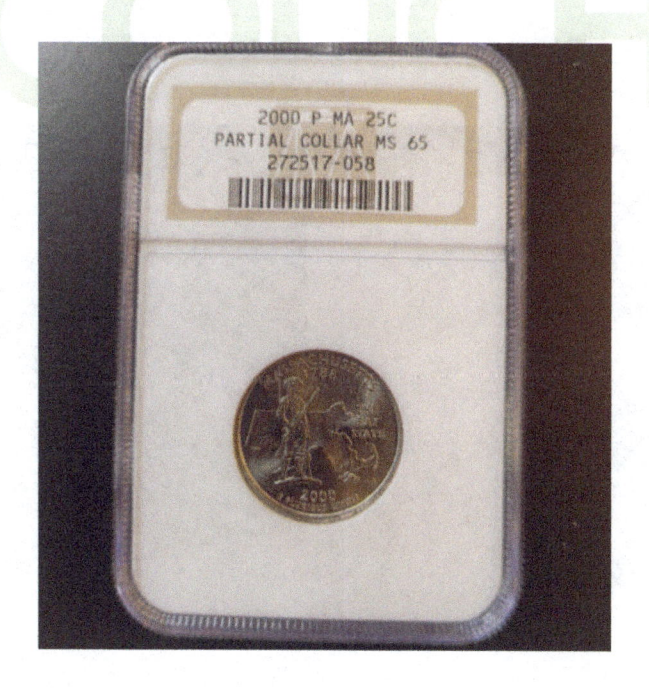

Error and Varieties
Split Die

This is an example of a split die taking place on a 1969 Roosevelt dime. This type of mint error can add a tremendous amount of value to your coins. *Images: Justin Couch*

Error and Varieties
Split Planchet

Split planchets occur when impurities are trapped in the metal causing the planchet to split apart. *Images: Justin Couch*

Strike Through

A "strike-through" coin is made when another object comes between a blank and a die at the time of striking.

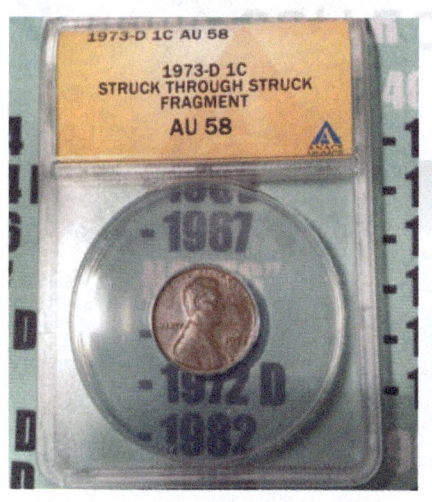

The above image shows a 1973 D Lincoln cent with a strike through error. You can see the error on the reverse of the penny. This coin was found coin roll hunting. *Images: Bryan Hooper*

Error and Varieties
Strike Through

This quarter has been nicknamed the "burning building" quarter of 2021 because of the strike through mint error placement on the quarter resembles a building on fire.
Image: Justin Couch

Images: Justin Couch

Error and Varieties
Strike Through

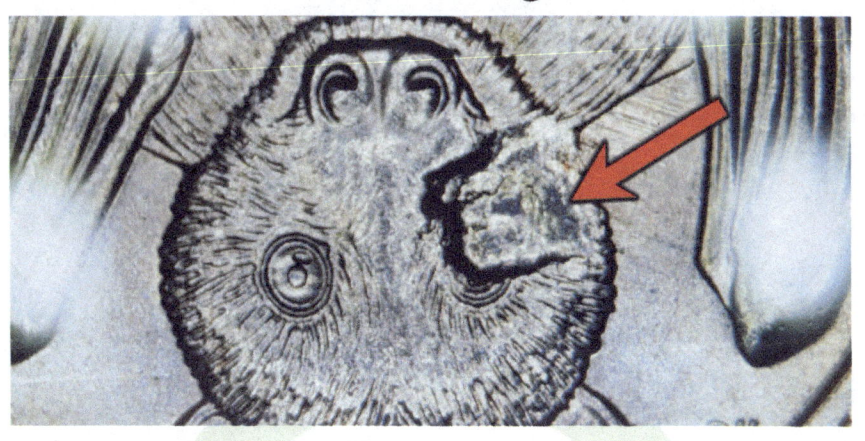

Some coin collectors found it interesting that a bat was featured on the reverse of the quarter during Covid in 2020. Look for a strike through mint error on the bats eye on these quarters. Some can big smaller or larger than others. ***Image: Justin Couch***

Images: Justin Couch

Error and Varieties
Strike Through

Couch Collectibles discovered this strike through mint error on a Lincoln wheat cent in a roll of pennies while coin roll hunting. ***Image: Justin Couch***

Strike Through

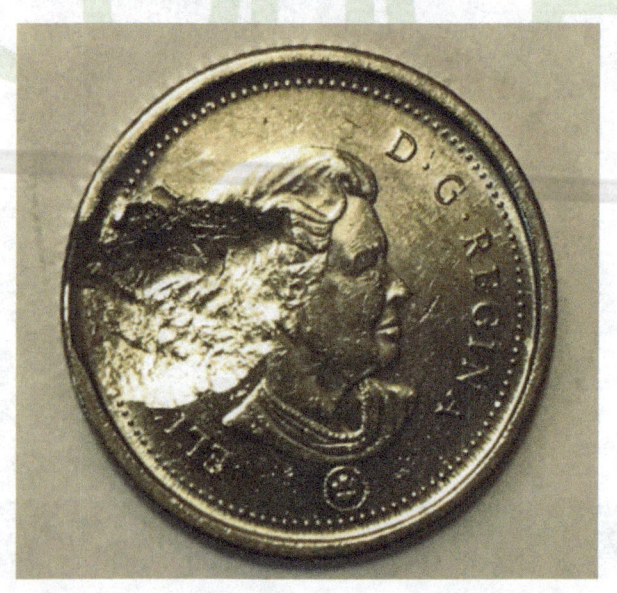

The above image shows a strike through mint error taking place on a Canadian coin discovered by Dan T, a subscriber and paid member of Couch Collectibles YouTube channel. ***Image: Dan T.***

Error and Varieties
Strike Through

On this 2022 quarter you will see a strike through mint error on the pony tail of Washington. This will add extra value to the quarter, so if you find one, keep it!
Image: Justin Couch

Error and Varieties
Strike Through

You will see a strike through mint error on the 2021 Lincoln cent in the image above. Be on the look out for these in your pocket change, coin jars, or even in coin rolls from the bank as this can add extra value to the coin. *Images: Justin Couch*

Error and Varieties
Saddle Strike

A saddle strike is created when a planchet or coin receives two simultaneous off-center strikes from two adjacent die pairs. ***Image: Chuck9999 eBay Seller***

"Woody" Lincoln Cent

A "woody" Lincoln cent will have a wood grain effect to the coin. This happens as a result of an improper alloy mix. You will see streaks on the penny in the above images. These are very common coins and they are not valuable unless they are a very high grade and specific date, however some collectors do enjoy adding them to their coin collections. ***Images: Sylvia Jimenez***

Error and Varieties
Waffled

Here is a 2003 P Missouri state quarter that is a Waffled mint error coin from Couch Collectibles coin collection. These coins are canceled by the mint using a machine the creates a waffled pattern because they do not meet the mint's standards.
Images: Justin Couch

Error and Varieties
2004 D Wisconsin Extra Low Leaf

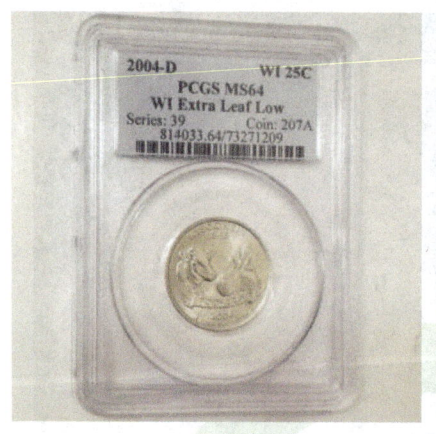

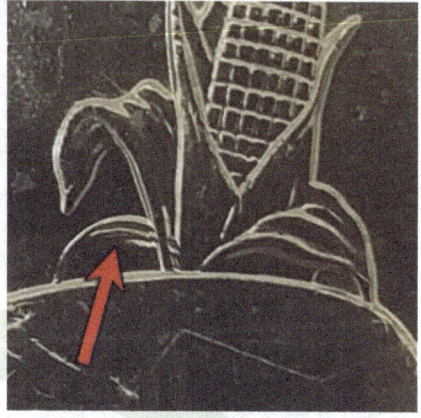

This is the extra low leaf Wisconsin state quarter from Couch Collectibles coin collection. This is a modern coin to look for from the bank or even in pocket change. Finding an extra leaf is the difficult part. Keep on searching and don't give up!
Images: Justin Couch

2004 D Wisconsin Extra Low & High Leaf

EXTRA LEAF LOW   **EXTRA LEAF HIGH**

The above image depicts the extra high leaf and low leaf Wisconsin quarter. You will notice the Wisconsin quarters you typically find will not have this high or low leaf. If you find one with the extra low or high leaf, you can definitely sell them and make a nice profit depending on the condition of the coin. ***Image courtesy of Professional Coin Grading Service (pcgs.com)***

Error and Varieties
2004 D Wisconsin Extra Low Leaf

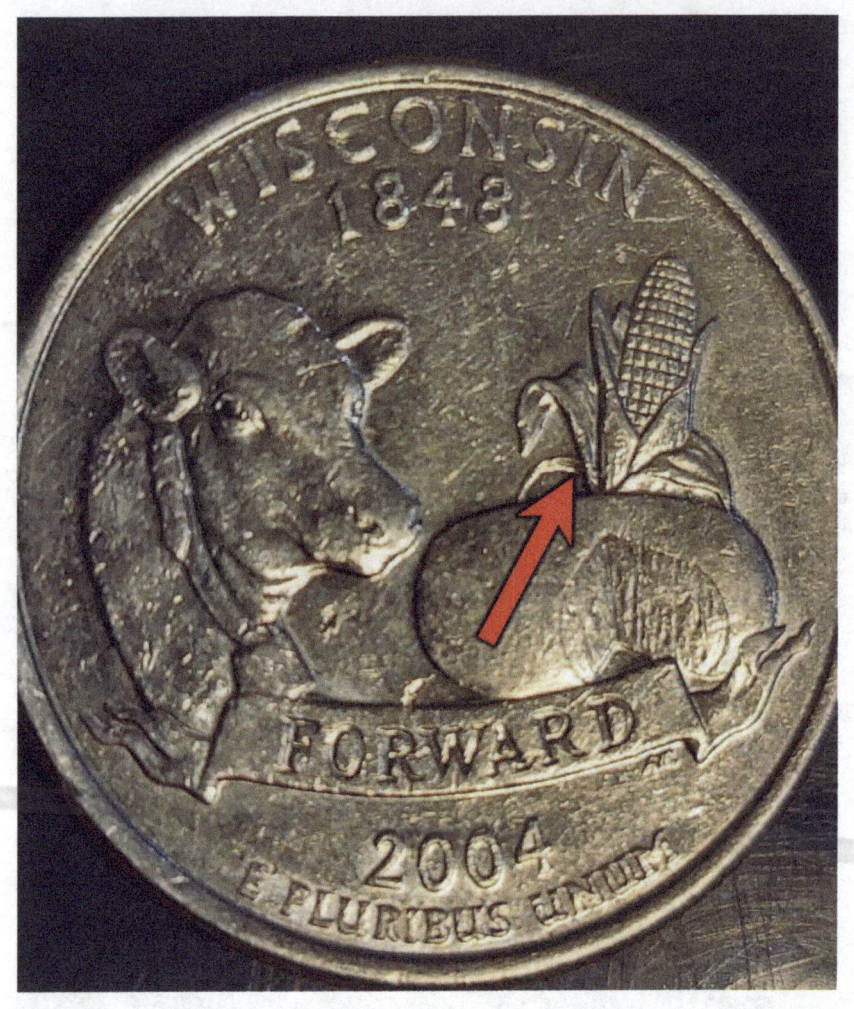

An extra low leaf version of the 2004 Wisconsin state quarter was discovered by a subscriber of Couch Collectibles YouTube channel. *Images: Mike G.*

Error and Varieties
Lincoln Cent No "FG" Initials

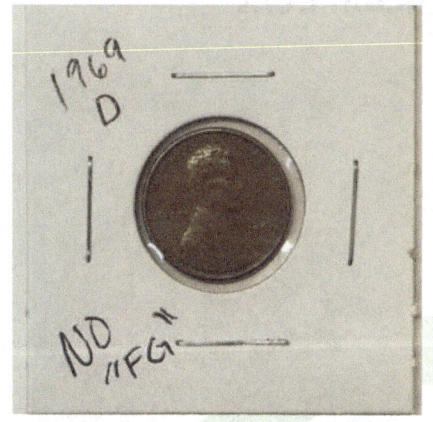

The above image is a 1969 D Lincoln cent that is missing the "FG" initials on the reverse of the coin. This coin is from Couch Collectibles coin collection. ***Images: Justin Couch***

Kennedy Half Dollar No "FG" Initials

Look for the missing "FG" initials on the reverse of the Kennedy half dollar coin. The picture on the left will show you what the FG initials look like and the image on the right will show you a Kennedy half dollar that is missing the FG initials. ***Images: Justin Couch, Sj's Mixed Adventures.***

140

Error and Varieties
Extra "V" Lincoln Cent

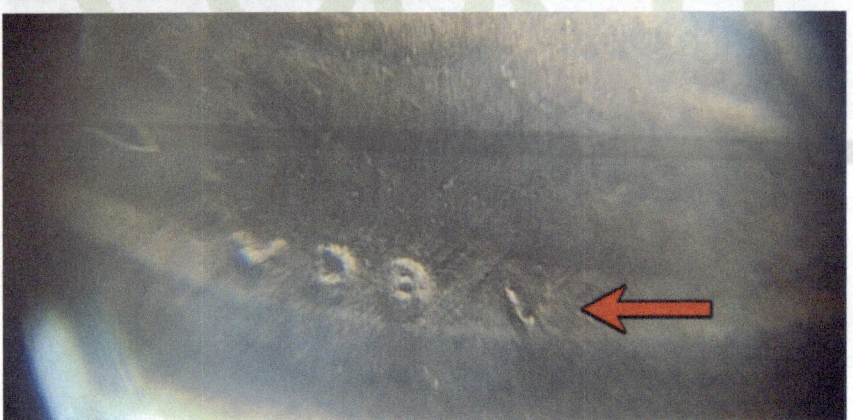

Look for the extra "V" to the right of the V.D.B initials on the obverse of the 2023 Lincoln cent. These coins have been selling for great money on the secondary market, especially the highest graded examples. *Images: Justin Couch*

BEST COIN COLLECTING SUPPLIES

COUCH COLLECTIBLES

DEALS

**COIN MICROSCOPES
COIN LOUPES
SILVER COINS
COIN MATS
COIN HUNTING CARDS
COIN SCALES
AND SO MUCH MORE!**

SOLO.TO/COUCHCOLLECTIBLES

SCAN ME

SCAN ME FOR DEALS

RPM'S, RPD'S, OMM'S, MPD'S

RPM (RE-PUNCHED MINT MARKS)

A repunched mint mark is created when the letter punch that is used to punch the mint mark into the working die leaves two or more offset impressions.

The above images displays a 1954 D Lincoln wheat cent with a repunched "D" mint mark. You can look for different types of RPM's on various different dates and denominations. You will see a list of repunched mint marks in the next several pages.
Images: Justin Couch

Here is a 1953 S Lincoln wheat cent with a repunched "S" mint mark. *Images: Justin Couch*

RPM'S, RPD'S, OMM'S, MPD'S

RPM (RE-PUNCHED MINT MARKS)

Here is a 1954 Lincoln wheat cent with a repunched D mint mark. *Images: Justin Couch*

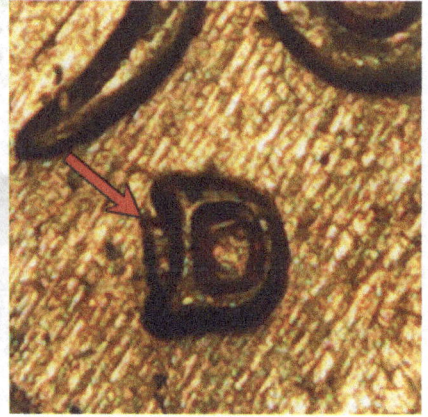

In the above image you will see a 1961 Lincoln cent with a D over a horizontal D mint mark. You can also look for these on Jefferson nickel D mint marks. *Images: Justin Couch*

RPM'S, RPD'S, OMM'S, MPD'S

RPM (RE-PUNCHED MINT MARKS)

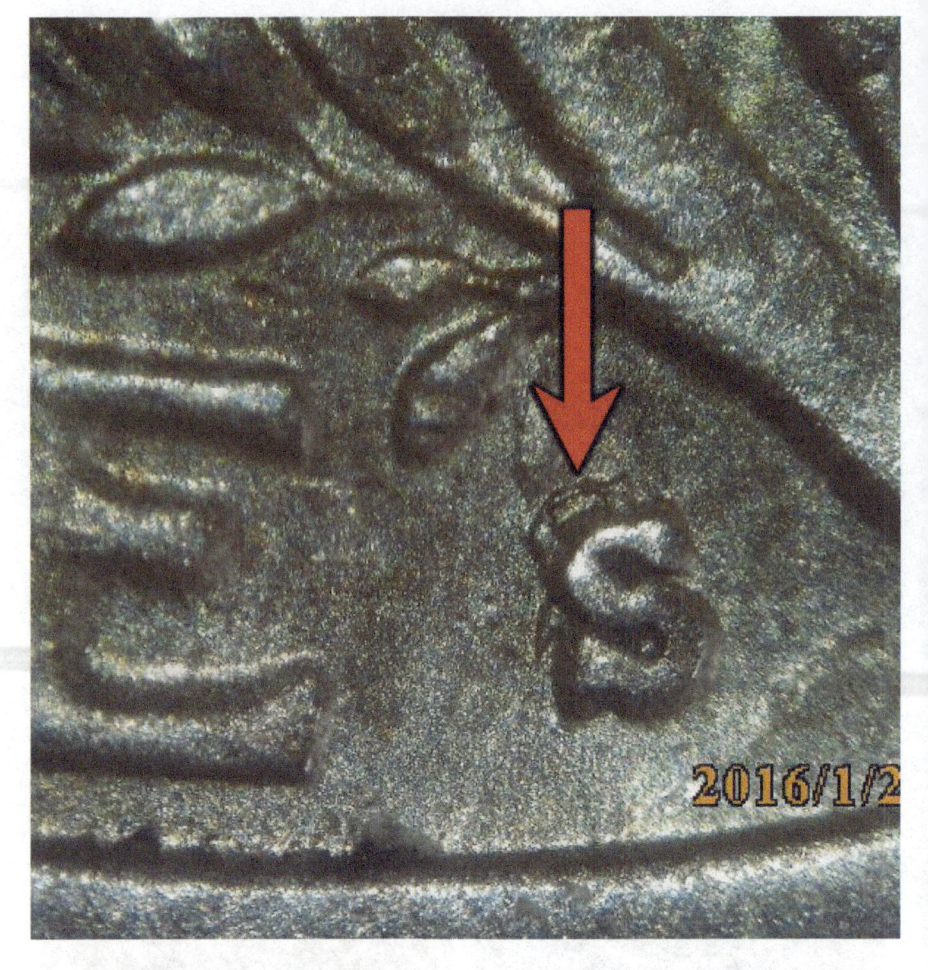

An absolutely amazing discovery by Emerson G. This is a re-punched "S" mint mark on a silver Mercury Dime. ***Image: Emerson G.***

RPM'S, RPD'S, OMM'S, MPD'S
RPD (REPUNCHED DATE)

A repunched date will have overlapping numbers of the date. These repunched dates with one or more numerals have been repunched into a master or working die.

Here is a 1864 Indian head cent with a repunched date (RPD). There are many different RPD's, especially on the Indian head pennies. You will see the "1" and "8" has been repunched. ***Images: Justin Couch***

RPM'S, RPD'S, OMM'S, MPD'S
OOM (OVER MINT MARK)

An over mint mark for an example would be a D/S, in which means a "D" mint mark is over an "S" mint mark. You can look for these on different denominations of coins. For an example you can look for a 1952 Lincoln cent with a D/S mint mark as well as a O/S silver Morgan dollar.

Here is an image of a 1951 D/S Lincoln cent. You will see the lower part of the "S" under the "D" mint mark. You can also see the "S" going through the middle inside of the "D". Again there will be many types of OMM's for different coins. **Images: Justin Couch**

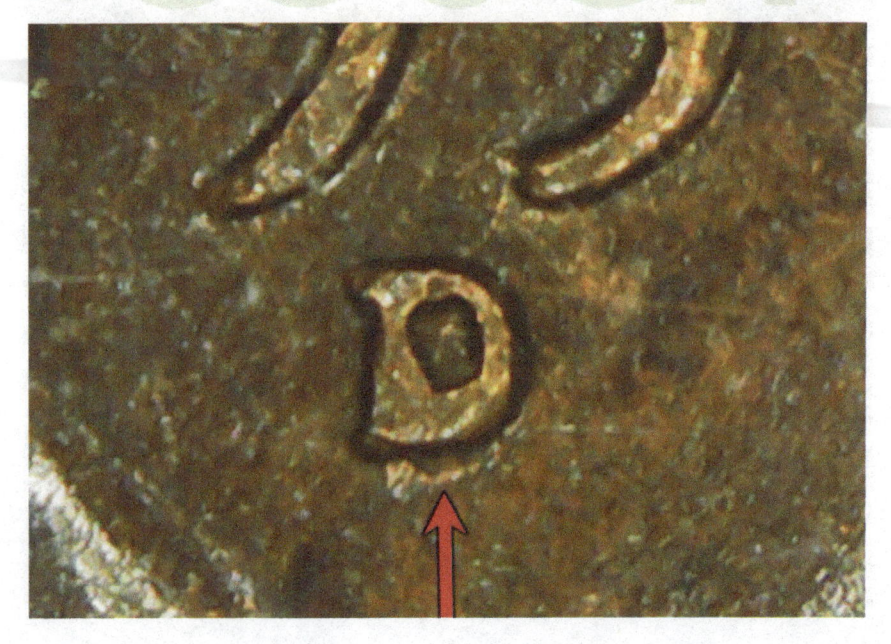

1942/1 Mercury Dime

1942 with a 2 over 1 on the Date

We looked at over mint marks and repunched mint marks but let's check out this amazing silver Mercury dime from Bryan Hooper's coin collection. You will notice the "2" of the date is over a "1". This is a super desirable coin. ***Images: Bryan Hooper***

Small Date / Large Date
SD vs LD

Over the next few pages you will see the difference between a small date and large date Lincoln cent. We will look at pennies from 1960, 1970, and 1982. You will notice here on the 1960 that the tail of the 6 on the large date is much longer than the 6 on the small date and the 0 on the small date is much skinnier. *Images: Justin Couch*

1960 D Small Date

1960 D Large Date

1960 D Small Date

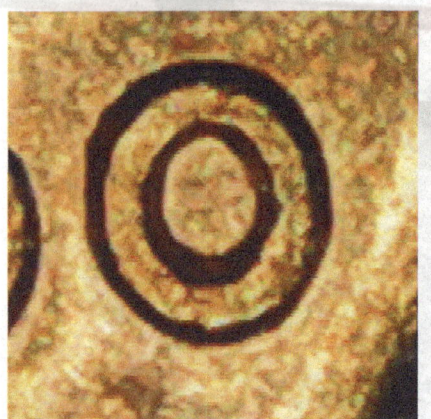

1960 D Large Date

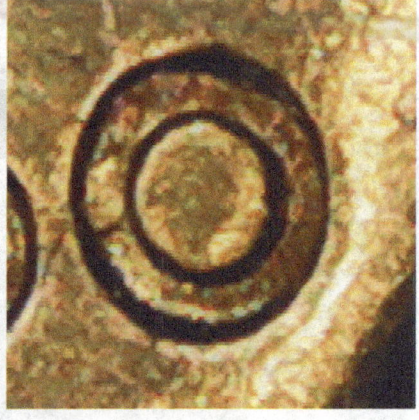

Small Date / Large Date

SD vs LD

The easiest way to tell the difference between the 1970 S small date and 1970 S large date is to look specifically at the "9" in the date. If the loop of the 9 bends sharply towards the 7, then it is a small date. Now if the loop is angled toward the top of the mint mark, then it is a large date penny.

1970 S Small Date   1970 S Large Date

SMALL DATE **LARGE DATE**

HIGH 7 **LOW 7**

Image courtesy of Professional Coin Grading Service (pcgs.com)

1970 S Small Date   1970 S Large Date

Image courtesy of Professional Coin Grading Service (pcgs.com)

Small Date / Large Date
SD vs LD

It is very easy to distinguish the difference between the 1982 small date and large date Lincoln cents. New collectors seem to still get these coins confused so I hope these images help. If you look at the "2" on the small date you will notice it has a curve in the middle of the "2" where as the large date "2" goes straight down without a curve. You want to look for the 1982 D small date copper that weighs 3.1 grams. *Images: Justin Couch*

1982 Small Date **1982 Large Date**

1982 Small Date 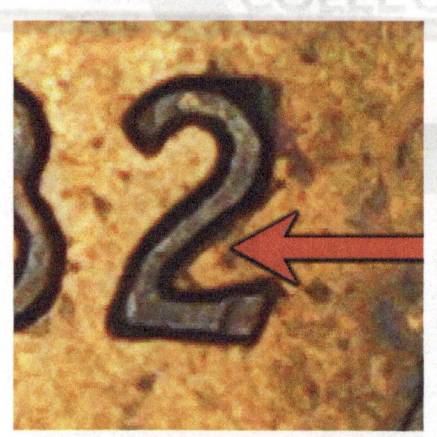 **1982 Large Date**

BEST COIN DEALS!

COINSTV™

DEALS

**SILVER COINS
COIN ROLLS
GRADED COINS
SILVER BAGS
ULTRA BREAKS
AND SO MUCH MORE!**

WWW.COINSTV.NET

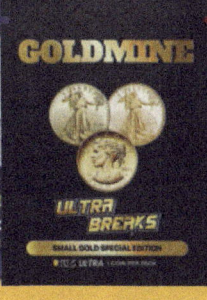

SCAN ME

SCAN
FOR $5 OFF $50

Abbreviations

Over the next several pages we will use abbreviated terms that you want to become familiar with.

7TF - This refers to the seven tail feathers on the reverse of the Morgan dollar.

8TF - This refers to the eight tail feathers on the reverse of the Morgan dollar.

CLOSE AM - This refers to the "AM" of the word America on the reverse of the Lincoln cent. You will notice the "A" and "M" are nearly touching.

DDO - A Doubled Die Obverse is essentially doubling taking place on the front, or rather the obverse of the coin.

DDR - A Doubled Die Reverse is essentially doubling taking place on the back, or rather the reverse of the coin.

MPD - This is a misplaced date.

NO "FG" - Look for missing "FG" initials on the reverse of the Lincoln cent as well as the Kennedy half dollar.

OBV - This is an abbreviation for "obverse" or the front of a coin.

OMM - An over mint mark for an example would be a D/S, in which means a "D" mint mark is over an "S" mint mark.

QDR - This is a quadruple die reverse.

REV - This is an abbreviation for "reverse" or the back of a coin.

RPD - The refers to a repunched date on a coin.

RPM - This refers to a repunched mint mark such as D/D or an S/S.

TDO - This is a triple die obverse.

TDR - This is a triple die reverse

WIDE AM - This refers to the "AM" of the word America on the reverse of the Lincoln cent. You will notice the "A" and "M" are spaced apart and are not touching.

Error Coin Dates

Indian Head Cent

1859/1859
1859/185
1859 18/18
1860 Pointed Bust
1861/61
1862 MPD
1862 DDR
1863/1863
1863 18/18
1863 MPD
1863 DDR
1864 DDO Bronze
1864/864 Bronze
1864/1864 Bronze
1864 Bronze Lathe Lines
1864 L Bronze (L on ribbon)
1864/1864 L Bronze
1864/186 L Bronze
1864 L 18/18 Bronze
1864 L 86/86 Bronze
1865 Plain
1865/18-5 Plain and Fancy 5
1865/1—5 Fancy 5
1865/186 Fancy 5
1865/1865 Fancy 5
1865 8/8 Fancy 5
1865 Fancy 5
1865 DDR Fancy 5
1866 DDO & MPD
1866/1—6
1866 1/1
1866/66
1866/18-6
1866 18/18
1867/67
1867 18/18
1867/18-7
1868 DDO
1868/868 DDO
1868/8 DDO & MPD
1868/1868
1868 MPD
1869/69
1869 18/18
1869/1869
1870/18-0 DDO
1870 8/8 DDO & MPD
1870 DDO & DDR
1870/187

1870 MPD & DDR
1870 18/18
1870 "PICK AXE"
1870 DDR
1870 REV OF 69
1871 7 and 1 Touching
1872/1872
1872/72
1872/872 MPD
1872 REV OF 69
1873 CLOSE 3
1873 DDO CLOSED 3
1873 OPEN 3
1873/73 OPEN 3
1873 MPD OPEN 3
1874 DDO
1875 18/18
1875/1—5
1875 18/18
1875 FILING LINES
1875 REVERSE DOT
1878 MPD
1878/8
1880 DDO & MDC
1882 MPD
1882 88/88
1882 BROKEN 2
1883 MPD
1883/1883/83
1883 MDC
1883 DDR
1884 MPD
1886 TYPE 1
1886/6 TYPE 1
1886 TYPE 2
1887 DDO
1887 MPD
1888/7
1888 88/88 MPD
1888 18/18
1888 88/88
1888/8
1888 MPD
1889/1889
1889/9 MPD
1889 DDR
1889 MDC
1890 TDO
1890 MPD

1891 DDO
1891/1891
1891 DDR
1892/8—2
1892 89/89
189S "SCARFACE"
1893 89/89
1893/3
1894/1894
1894 MPD
1895/895
1895/1895
1896/6
1897 MPD
1897 89/89
1898/898
1898/98
1898 MPD
1899/1899
1899 9/9 CHIPPED 9
1899/1—9
1899/99
1900/0
1900/9—0
1900 90/90
1901/1—1
1901/1901
1902 EYE GOUGE
1903 MPD
1903 1/1
1903/1903
1904/1—4
1905/5
1906/06
1906 0/0 MPD
1906/190
1906 MPD
1907/907 MPD
1907 90/90
1907/190
1907 90/90
1907 MPD
1907/1907
1907/07
1908 MPD
1908 MPD

Error Coin Dates

Lincoln Wheat Cent

1909 VDB DDO
1909 S/S
1909 S/HOR S
1910 S/S
1911 D/D
1911 D/D/D
1911 S/S
1917 DDO
1922 D WEAK D
1922 NO D STRONG REVERSE
1922 NO D WEAK REVERSE
1924 S/S
1925 S/S
1927 DDO
1927 D/D
1928 S SMALL S
1928 S LARGE S
1928 S LARGE S/S
1929 S/S
1930 D/D
1930 S/S
1934 DDO
1934 D/D/D/D
1934 D/D
1935 DDO
1936 DDO
1937 D/D
1938 D/D
1938 S/S
1938 S/S/S
1939 DDO
1940 D/D
1940 S/S
1941 DDO
1941 S SMALL S
1941 S LARGE S
1941 S/S LARGE S
1942 DDO
1942 D/D
1942 S/S DDO
1942 S/S/S
1942 S/S
1943 DDO
1943 BRONZE
1943 D/D
1943 D BRONZE
1943 S DDO
1943 S BRONZE

1944 D DDO
1944 D/D
1944 D/S
1945 DDO
1945 S/S
1946 D/D
1946 S INVERTED S
1946 S/D
1946 S/S
1947 DDO
1947 S/S
1949 D/D/D
1949 S DDO
1949 S/S
1950 D/D
1950 S/S
1951 D DDO
1951 D/D
1951 D/S
1952 D/S
1952 D/D
1953 D/D
1953 S/S
1954 D/D/D
1954 D/D
1954 S/S
1955 DDO
1955 D DDO
1955 S/S
1955 S/S/S
1956 D/D
1957 D DDO
1957 D/D/D
1957 D/D
1958 DDO
1958 D/D/D

155

Error Coin Dates

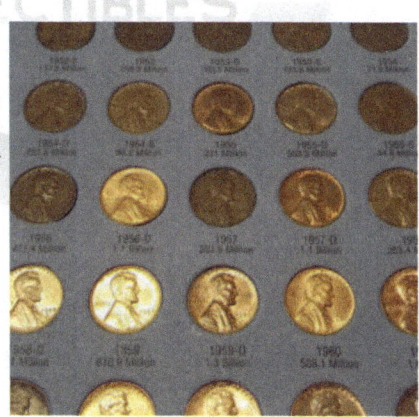

Lincoln Cent

1959 DDO
1959 D/D/D
1959 D/D
1959 with Wheat Cent reverse
1960 SMALL DATE
1960 DDO SM/LG DATE PROOF
1960 DDO LG/SM DATE PROOF
1960 TDO LG/SM DATE
1960 LARGE DATE
1960 D/D SM/LG DATE
1960 D/D LARGE DATE
1961 D/HORIZ D
1961 D/D
1962 DDO PROOF
1963 D DDO
1963 DDR PROOF
1964 D DDR
1964 D/D
1966 DDO
1966 DDR
1968 DDO
1968 DDO
1968 D/D
1968 D DDR
1968 S DDO PROOF
1969 D NO "FG"
1969 S DDO
1970 S SMALL DATE
1970 S LARGE DATE
1970 S DDO SMALL DATE
1970 S DDO LG/SM DATE PROOF
1970 S TDO LARGE DATE PROOF
1970 S DDO LARGE DATE PROOF
1970 S DDO LARGE DATE
1970 S/S LARGE DATE
1971 DDO
1971 S DDO PROOF
1972 DDO
1972 D DDO
1972 S DDO PROOF
1980 DDO
1982 LG DT BRONZE DDO
1982 SM DT BRONZE TRANSITIONAL
1982 SM DT ZINC DDR
1983 DDO
1983 DDR
1984 DDO

1984 D DDO
1987 D/D
1988 DDO
1988 REV OF 89
1988 D REV OF 89
1990 PROOF NO "S"
1992 CLOSE "AM"
1992 D CLOSE "AM"
1994 DDR
1995 DDO
1995 D DDO
1996 DDO
1997 DDO
1998 S CLOSE "AM"
1998 WIDE "AM"
1999 S CLOSE "AM"
1999 WIDE "AM"
2000 WIDE "AM"
2004 DDR
2006 DDO
2014 DDO
2015 DDO
2018 D DDO (Ear)
2019 DDO
2023 Extra "V"

Error Coin Dates

Two Cent Piece

1864 LARGE MOTTO DDO
1864/1864 LG MOTTO
1864/186 LG MOTTO
1864 1/1 LG MOTTO
1864 LG MOTTO DIE CLASH
1865 DDO PLAIN 5
1865/1865 PLAIN 5
1865 18/18 PLAIN 5
1865/1865 FANCY 5
1865/1--5 FANCY 5
1865 86/86 FANCY 5
1865 MPD FANCY 5
1866 DDR
1867 DDO
1868 MPD
1868/1868
1869 18/18 MPD
1869 18/18
1870 DDO
1871 DDO
1871/1871
1872 DDO

Error Coin Dates

Silver Three Cent Piece
1851 18/18
1851/851
1852 1/INVERTED 2
1852/52
1852 DDR
1853 18/18
1853/1--3
1854 85/85
1855/855
1862/1

Error Coin Dates

Nickel Three Cent Piece
1865 DDO
1865/5 MPD
1865/1865
1865 MPD
1865/65
1866 DDO
1866/866
1869 18/18
1869/1869
1869 DDR
1870/1870 DDO
1870 MPD
1870 MPD & DDR
1871 TDO
1873 18/18 CLOSED 3
1875 MPD
1881/81
1881 88/88
1889/89

Error Coin Dates

Liberty Head V Nickel

1883 8/1 NO CENTS
1883/1883 NO CENTS
1883 1/1 NO CENTS
1883 8/1 CENTS
1884/188
1886/1-86
1887 DDR
1888/188 DDO
1889 18/18
1890/189
1897/1897
1898/189
1898/898
1898 1/1
1899/9
1899/1899
1900 DDR
1903/903
1907/19/9
1908/08
1908 1/1

Error Coin Dates

Buffalo Nickel

1913 TYPE 1 3 ½ LEGS
1913 TYPE 1 3 ½ LEGS 2 FEATHERS
1913 D TYPE 1 2 FEATHERS
1913 S TYPE 1 2 FEATHERS NO "F"
1913 DDO TYPE 2
1913 DDR TYPE 2
1913 DDR TYPE 2
1914 S/S
1915 DDO
1915 2 FEATHERS
1915 D 2 FEATHERS
1915 D/D
1915 S/S/S
1916 DDO
1916 NO "F"
1916 2 FEATHERS
1917 2 FEATHERS
1917 NO "F"
1917 DDR
1917 D 2 FEATHERS
1917 D 3 ½ LEGS
1917 S 2 FEATHERS
1918 2 FEATHERS
1918 DDR
1918/7 D
1918 S 2 FEATHERS
1919 DDO
1919 NO "F"
1919 2 FEATHERS
1919 NO "F" 2 FEATHERS
1919 S 2 FEATHERS
1920 2 FEATHERS
1920 D 2 FEATHERS
1920 D/D
1920 S 2 FEATHERS
1921 2 FEATHERS
1921 S 2 FEATHERS
1923 2 FEATHERS
1925 D 2 FEATHERS
1925 S 2 FEATHERS
1925 S/S
1926 DDO & DDR
1926 D 2 FEATHERS
1926 D 3 ½ LEGS
1927 D/D/D
1927 D 3 ½ LEGS
1927 S DDO
1927 S 2 FEATHERS
1928 S 2 FEATHERS
1929 DDO
1929 S 2 FEATHERS
1929 S/S/S
1929 S/S
1930 DDO
1930 DDR
1930 S DDO
1930 S 2 FEATHERS
1930 S/S
1931 S DDR
1931 S TDR
1931 S/S
19334 D SMALL D
1934 D LARGE D
1935 DDR
1935 D/D/D/D
1935 D/D
1935 S/S
1935 S/S/S
1935 S DDR
1936 DDO
1936 DDR
1936 D 3 ½ LEGS
1936 D/D
1936 S/S
1937 D/D
1937 S/S
1938 D/D
1938 D/S
1938 D/D/D/S

1918   1918-D

Error Coin Dates

Jefferson Nickel

1938 DDO
1938 QDO
1938 D DDO
1939 REV OF 38
1939 REV OF 40
1939 DDR REV OF 40
1939 QDR REV OF 40
1939 D REV OF 38
1939 D DDO REV OF 38
1939 D REV OF 40
1939 S REV OF 38
1939 S REV OF 40
1940 S/S
1941 D/D
1941 S SMALL S
1941 S LARGE S
1941 S/S LARGE S
1942 DDO
1942 D/HORIZ D
1942 D/D
1942 P/P SILVER
1942 P/P/P SILVER
1942 S/S/S SILVER
1942 S/S SILVER
1943/2 P SILVER
1943 P DDO SILVER
1943 P/P SILVER
1943 P/P/P SILVER
1943 D/D SILVER
1944 P/P SILVER
1944 D/D SILVER
1944 S/S SILVER
1945 P/P SILVER
1945 P DDR SILVER
1945 P TDR SILVER
1945 P/P/P TDR SILVER
1945 P TDR SILVER
1945 P DDR SILVER
1945 D DDO SILVER
1945 D/D SILVER
1945 D/D/D SILVER
1946 DDR
1946 D/INVERT D
1946 D/D
1946 S DDO
1949 D/S
1951 DDO PROOF

1953 DDO PROOF
1953 D/INVERT D
1954 D/D
1954 S/D
1954 S/S
1954 S DDR
1955 TDR PROOF
1955 D/S
1956 DDO PROOF
1956 QDR
1956 TDR
1957 QDO PROOF
1958 D/INVERT D
1960 QDR PROOF
1962 DDR
1963 TDR
1964 TDR PROOF
1964 DDO
1964 D/D
1968 S DDO PROOF
1968 S/S PROOF
1969 S/S PROOF
1971 S DDR PROOF
1971 NO "S" PROOF
1975 D MISPLACED MINT MARK
1990 S DDO PROOF
2004 P HANDSHAKE DDO
2005 P BISON DDO
2005 D BISON (SPEARED)

1940-D 1940-S 1941

1942 1942-D 1942-P

Error Coin Dates

Liberty Seated Dime

1837 LD DATE DIE CRACKED & CLASHED
1837 SM DATE REVERSE CRACKED
1838 O/O
1838 SMALL STARS DDR, OBVERSE CRACKED
1838 LARGE STARS DDR
1838 LARGE STARS REVERSE CRACKED
1838 LARGE STARS OBVERSE CRACKED
1838 PARTIAL DRAPERY
1838 PARTIAL DRAPERY RPD & REVERSE CLASHED
1839 OBVERSE SHATTERED
1839 O LARGE O BOTH DIES CRACKED
1839 O LARGE O/O
1839 O LARGE O REVERSE SHATTERED
1839 O VERY LARGE O OBV LDS & REV OF
1840 NO DRAPERY CHIN WHISKERS
1840 O NO DRAPERY MEDIUM O & CRACKED REVERSE
1841/184 REVERSE CRACKED
1841/841 REVERSE CRUMBLING
1841 O LARGE O CLOSED BUD REVERSE
1841 O SMALL O CLOSED BUD REVERSE
1842 OBVERSE RIM CUD
1842 O SMALL O OBVERSE RIM CUD
1842 O MEDIUM O REVERSE SHATTERED
1843/1843
1845/1845 REVERSE CRACKED
1847 DATE OVERLAPS BASE
1848/48
1849/8--9
1849/184 O SMALL O
1851/851 MPD REVERSE RUSTED
1852/52 REVERSE CRACKED
1853 NO ARROWS OBVERSE CLASHED
1853/1853 ARROWS
1853 O ARROWS OBVERSE SHATTERED
1854 ARROWS OBVERSE SHATTERED
1854 O ARROWS OBVERSE SHATTERED
1854 O ARROWS OBLIQUE O OBVERSE CRACKED
1855/1855 ARROWS DDO
1855 DDO ARROWS
1856/185 DDO SMALL DATE
1856 DDO SMALL DATE
1856/56 O LARGE O
1856/1--56 O LARGE O
1857 O REVERSE SHATTERED
1859 MPD
1860 DDO

163

Error Coin Dates

Liberty Seated Dime

1861 TYPE 1 OBVERSE RUSTED
1861 TYPE 2 REVERSE RUSTED
1862/2 DDO REVERSE GOUGED
1868 18/18
1870/0
1872/2
1872 MPD
1872/18-2
1872 DDR
1873/1873 NO ARROWS
1873 ARROWS DDO
1874/74 ARROWS
1874 ARROWS, FAINT ARROWS
1875 MPD OBVERSE CLASHED
1875 CC BELOW BOW BOTH DIES CLASHED
1875 CC ABOVE BOW, BOTH DIES CRACKED
1875 S BELOW BOW, MPD & CLEAR MICRO S
1875 S ABOVE BOW REVERSE SHATTERED
1876 DDR TYPE 1 REVERSE
1876 CC DDO TYPE 1 REVERSE
1876 18/18 CC REVERSE DDR
1876 CC MPD TYPE 1 REVERSE DDR
1876 DDR TYPE 1 REVERSE
1876/1--6 S TYPE 1 REVERSE, REVERSE CRACKED
1876/187
1877 MPD TYPE 2 REVERSE
1877/1876 CC TYPE 2 REVERSE
1877 18/18
1878 CC REVERSE SHATTERED
1879/18--9
1879
1882/18-2
1883 BROKEN 3
1886/86
1887 S/S
1888/8 MPD
1888 S/S
1888 S/S MPD
1889/1889 MPD
1889 8/8 DDR
1889 DDR
1889/1--9 DDR
1890 MPD
1890 S/S MEDIUM S
1890 S MPD
1891 DDO
1891/891
1891 89/89
1891 MPD
1891 O
1891 O REVERSE DIE SHATTERED
1891 89/89 O/O
1891 O/HORIZ O
1891 89/89 O/S
1891 O/S
1891 S MED/SM S

Error Coin Dates

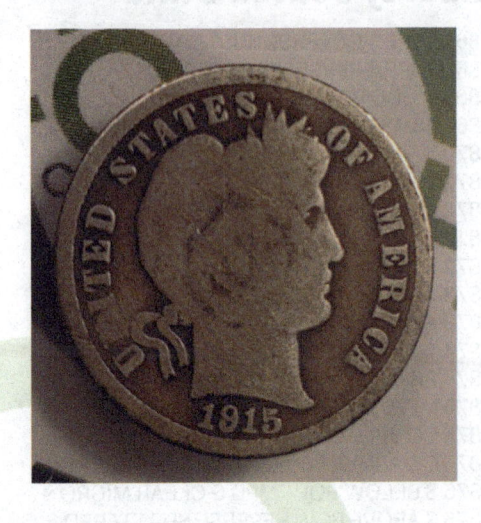

Barber Dime

1892/892
1892/1892
1892/1892 O
1893 S/S
1895/95
1896/896
1897/1897
1897/897
1897 8/8
1898/1898
1899/9 O
1899 O/O
1901 O/HORIZ O
1903 1/1
1903/3
1903/3 O
1903/1903 O
1906/906 MPD
1906/1906 O
1907 19/19
1907 O/O
1908/908
1908/1908
1908 90/90
1908/08 D
1908/8 D
1908 D MPD
1912 D/D
1914 D/D
1915 S/S

Error Coin Dates

Mercury Dime

1919 DDO
1926 DDO
1928 S SMALL S
1928 S LARGE S
1929 S DDO
1931 D DDO & DDR
1931 S DDO
1934 D SMALL D
1934 D LARGE D
1934 D/D LARGE D
1935 DDO
1935 S/S
1936 DDO
1937 DDO
1937 S DDO
1938 D/D
1939 DDO
1939 D/D
1940 D/D
1940 S DDO & DDR
1940 S/S
1941 DDO
1941 D DDO & DDR
1941 D/D
1941 S SMALL S
1941 S/S SMALL S
1941 S LARGE S
1942/41
1942 D/D
1943 D/D
1943 S/S/S
1943 S TRUMPET S
1944 D DDO
1944 D/D
1945 DDO
1945 D/D
1945 D/HORIZ D
1945 S MICRO S
1945 S TRUMPET S
1945 S/ HORIZ S
1945 S/S/S
1945 S/S

The 1916 D Mercury dime is the rarest Mercury dime ever minted because they only struck 264,000 of these coins. They are valuable in any type of condition. The example above is estimated to be a $1,000.00 coin.

Error Coin Dates

Roosevelt Dime

1946 DDO & DDR
1946 DDO
1946 DDR
1946 D/D
1946 S/S DDO
1946 S/S/S DDR
1946 S/S DDR
1946 S/S/S
1946 S/S
1946 S SANS SERIF
1947 DDO
1947 D DDO
1947 S/D SANS SERIF
1947 S/D TRUMPET S
1947 S/S
1947 S DDR
1948 DDR
1948 S/S
1950 DDR PROOF
1950 D DDR
1950 S/INVERT S
1950 S/S
1951 D/D
1953 D/HORIZ D
1953 S/S
1954 DDO PROOF
1954 DDR
1954 S/S
1954 S NO "JS"
1955 S/S
1956 DDO PROOF
1959 D/INVERT D
1959 D/D
1960 DDO PROOF
1960 DDR PROOF
1960 D/D
1961 D DDR
1962 D/HORIZ D
1962 D/D
1963 DDR PROOF
1963 DDO
1963 DDR
1963 D/D
1963 D DDR
1964 DDO BLUNT 9 PROOF
1964 POINT 9
1964 BLUNT 9
1964 DDR BLUNT 9

1964 D POINTED 9
1964 D BLUNT 9
1964 D/D POINTED 9
1964 D DDO BLUNT 9
1964 D/D BLUNT 9
1964 D DDR BLUNT 9
1966 SMS DDR
1967 DDO
1968 S DDO PROOF
1968 S/S PROOF
1968 S DDR PROOF
1968 NO "S" PROOF
1968 DDO
1969 REV OF 68
1969 D/D
1970 S DDR PROOF
1970 NO "S" PROOF
1970 DDR
1970 REV OF 68
1970 D DDR
1970 D REV OF 68
1975 S/S PROOF
1975 NO "S" PROOF
1982 NO "P"
1982 NO "P" WEAK STRIKE
2004 D EAR GOUGE

1946   1946-D

1947-S   1948

Error Coin Dates

Seated Liberty Quarter

1840 O NO DRAPERY
1840/0 O NO DRAPERY
1841 O DDO
1843 18/18
1845/845
1846/46
1847 MPD
1847/47 DDR
1847 DDR
1848/1--8
1848/1848
1850 MPD
1852/852
1853/53 NO ARROWS
1853/854 ARR & RAYS
1853 O/HORIZ O ARR & RAYS
1855 ARROWS DDO
1856 MPD
1856 S LG/SM S
1857 MPD
1857 CLASHED WITH CENT REVERSE
1857 SMOKING LIBERTY
1857 O MPD
1858 CLASHED WITH CENT REVERSE
1872/1872
1875 MPD
1876 MPD
1876 18/11
1876/6 TYPE 2 REVERSE
1876 MPD TYPE 2 REVERSE
1876/1-76 TYPE 2 REVERSE
1876/1876 CC TYPE 1 REVERSE
1876 CC REV OF 73CC
1876/6 CC TYPE 2 REVERSE
1876 S MPD
1877/77 CC
1877 S/HORIZ S
1891 MPD

Error Coin Dates

Standing Liberty Quarter

1917 D TYPE 1 DDR
1918/7
1920 S "TEARDROP"
1926 S "TEARDROP"
1928 D/D
1928 S/S LARGE S
1929 S/S

Error Coin Dates

Barber Quarter
1892 TDR TYPE 1 REVERSE
1892 DDO TYPE 2 REVERSE
1892 8/8 TDO TYPE 2 REVERSE
1892 TDO TYPE 2 REVERSE
1892 TDR TYPE 2 REVERSE
1892 O/O TYPE 1 REVERSE
1892 O DDO TYPE 2 REVERSE
1892/1892 O TYPE 2 REVERSE
1892 O DDR TYPE 2 REVERSE
1892 S/S
1892 S TDR TYPE 1 REVERSE
1895 S/S
1899 DDR
1902 O MPD
1907/1907 D DDO
1907 S/S
1908 D MPD
1908 O MPD
1914 D DDO
1916 D/D

Error Coin Dates

Washington Quarter

1932 DDO
1934 LIGHT MOTTO
1934 MEDIUM MOTTO
1934 DDO
1934 MEDIUM MOTTO DDO
1934 HEAVY MOTTO
1934 D SM D MEDIUM MOTTO
1934 D LG D MEDIUM MOTTO
1934 D SM D HEAVY MOTTO
1934 D LG D HEAVY MOTTO
1935 DDO
1936 DDO
1936 S/S
1937 DDO
1938 DDO
1939 DDO
1939 D/D
1939 S DDO
1940 D DDO
1940 D/D
1940 D/D/D
1940 S/S
1940 S/S/S
1941 DDO
1941 DDR
1941 D DDO
1941 D DDR
1941 S SMALL S
1941 S LARGE TRUMPET S
1941 S LARGE SERIF S
1942 DDO
1942 DDR
1942 D DDO
1942 D DDR
1942 D/D 1943 DDO
1943 D DDO
1943 D/D DDO
1943 S DDO
1943 S "GOITER"
1943 S TRUMPET
1943 S/S
1944 DDO
1944 D DDO
1944 D/D
1944 S DDO
1945 DDO
1945 S DDO
1945 S/S
1946 DDO

1946 DDR
1946 D/D
1946 S/S
1947 DDO
1947 S/S
1947 S/S/S
1948 S/S/S/S
1949 D/S
1950 DDR
1950 D/D
1950 D/S
1950 D DDR
1950 S/S
1950 S/D
1950 S DDR
1951 D DDO
1951 D/D
1952 D DDO
1952 D LARGE D
1952 S/S
1953 DDO PROOF
1953 D/INVERT D
1953 D/S
1953 D DDR
1956 TYPE B REV
1956 D/INVERT D
1956 D DDR
1957 TYPE B REV
1958 TYPE B REV
1959 DDO PROOF
1959 TYPE B REV
1960 DDR PROOF
1960 TYPE B REV
1961 DDO PROOF
1961 TYPE B REV
1961 D/D
1962 DDO
1962 TYPE B REV
1963 DDR PROOF
1963 DDO
1964 DDO & DDR
1963 DDO
1963 DDR
1963 TYPE B REV
1963 D DDO
1964 DDR
1964 TYPE B REV
1964 D DDO
1964 D/D

Error Coin Dates

Washington Quarter

1964 D DDR
1964 D TYPE C REV OF 65
1965 DDO
1965 DDR
1966 DDR
1967 SMS DDO PROOF
1968 S DDO PROOF
1968 S/S PROOF
1968 S DDR PROOF
1968 D DDR
1969 S DDO PROOF
1969 S/S/S PROOF
1969 D/D
1969 D TYPE H REV
1970 S DDR PROOF
1970 D DDO
1970 D DDR
1970 D TYPE H REV
1971 DDR
1971 D DDR
1971 D TYPE H REV
1972 TYPE H REV
1776-1976 S SILVER DDO PROOF
1776-1976 D DDO
1776-1976 D DDO
1983 P SPITTING EAGLE
1990 S DDO PROOF
2009 DISTRICT OF COLUMBIA DDR
2015 HOMESTEAD DDR
2020 P DDO (SALT RIVER BAY)

Error Coin Dates

Barber Half Dollar

1892 TDR
1893 TDR
1907 S/S
1909 S INVERTED S
1911 S/S

COIN MICROSCOPES AVAILABLE AT https://www.solo.to/couchcollectibles

Error Coin Dates

Walking Liberty Half Dollar

1916 D/D
1917 D OBVERSE
1917 D REVERSE
1917 S OBVERSE
1917 S REVERSE
1918 D NO "AW"
1928 S SMALL S
1928 S LARGE S
1929 S NO "AW"
1933 S DDO
1934 D SMALL D
1934 D LARGE D
1936 DDO
1939 D DDO
1939 D/D
1941 NO "AW" PROOF
1941 NO "AW"
1941 D/D
1941 S/S
1942 DDO
1942 DDR
1942 D/D
1942 S SMALL S
1942 S LARGE S
1942 S LARGE TRUMPET S
1942 S DDO TRUMPET S
1942 S LARGE SERIF S
1942 S NO "AW"
1944 NO "AW"
1944 D HAND CUT "AW"
1944 S/S
1945 "SUNBURST"
1945 NO "AW"
1945 D NO "AW"
1946 DDO
1946 DDR
1946 S/S

In the image below you will see the "AW" initials on the reverse of the Walking Liberty half dollar coin. You want to look for these coins that are missing the "AW" initials. ***Images: Justin Couch***

Error Coin Dates

Fraklin Half Dollar
1948 DDR
1948 D/D
1948 D DDR
1949 S/S
1950 QDO PROOF
1950 D/D
1951 DDR PROOF
1951 "BUGS BUNNY"
1951 S/S
1951 S DDR
1952 "BUGS BUNNY" PROOF
1952 RECUT HAIR PROOF
1952 S/S/S
1953 S/S
1954 DDO PROOF
1955 DDO PROOF
1955 DDR PROOF
1955 "BUGS BUNNY"
1956 TYPE 1 DDR PROOF
1956 TYPE 2 DDO PROOF
1956 TYPE 2 DDR PROOF
1956 "BUGS BUNNY"
1957 TDR PROOF
1957 D/D
1959 DDR
1960 DDO PROOF
1960 DDO
1961 DDO PROOF
1961 DDR PROOF
1961 D/D
1962 DDO PROOF
1962 "D" ON BELL PROOF
1962 D/D

Error Coin Dates

Kennedy Half Dollar
1964 ACCENT HAIR PROOF
1964 ACCENT HAIR DDO PROOF
1964 ACCENT HAIR QDR PROOF
1964 TYPE 1 REVERSE STRAIGHT "G"
1964 DDO PROOF
1964 QDO PROOF
1964 TDO PROOF
1964 DDO
1964 DDR
1964 D DDO
1964 D TDO
1964 D QDO
1964 D/D
1964 D/HORIZ D
1965 SMS DDR PROOF
1965 DDR
1966 SMS DDO PROOF
1966 SMS NO "FG"
1966 DDO
1967 SMS NO "F"
1967 DDO
1967 DDR
1968 S DDO PROOF
1968 S/S PROOF
1968 S SERIF S/KNOB S PROOF
1968 S INVERTED S PROOF
1968 S DDR PROOF
1970 S DDO PROOF
1971 S DDO PROOF
1971 D DDO
1972 DDO
1972 D NO "FG"
1973 D DDO
1974 D DDO
1776-1976 S CLAD DDR PROOF
1776-1976 S SILVER DDO
1977 D DDO
1982 P NO "FG"
1983 P NO "FG"
1988 S DDO PROOF
1988 P NO "FG"
1992 S DDO SILVER PFOOF
2018 S SILVER LIGHT FINISH REVERSE PROOF SET
2023 P DDO

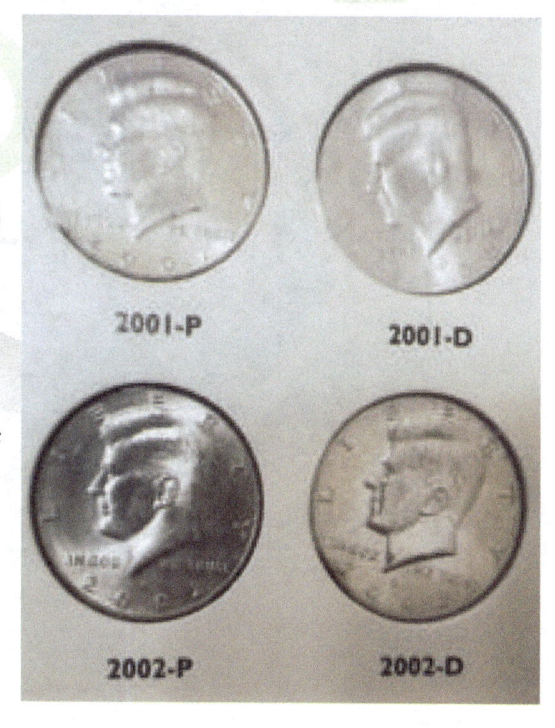

176

Error Coin Dates

Seated Liberty Dollar

1859 18/18
1868 MPD
1869 MPD
1871 MPD
1872 MPD

Error Coin Dates

Morgan Dollar

1878 8TF
1878 8TF OBVERSE CLASH
1878 8TF DDO "RIB"
1878 8TF STICK FEATHER
1878 8TF FRIST DIE MARRIAGE
1878 8TF CONCAVE REVERSE
1878 8TF SPIKED "A"
1878 8TF DOUBLED EAR
1878 8TF EYE SPIKES
1878 8TF DDO PROFILE
1878 8TF BOLL LINES
1878 8TF DDO "LIBERTY"
1878 8TF DOUBLED DATE
1878 8TF WEAK "LIB"
1878 8TF "LIB" & CLASH
1878 8TF "LIB" & BREAKS
1878 8TF DDO LIPS
1878 7/8TF STRONG
1878 7/8TF WEAK
1878 7TF REV OF 78
1878 7TF DDO "RIB"
1878 7TF DISCONNECTED LEAF
1878 7TF LOW "8"
1878 7TF DASH "8"
1878 7TF TDO BLOSSOMS
1878 7TF DDO "P"
1878 7TF TDO STAR
1878 7TF SOFT PACK
1878 7TF SPIKED EYE
1878 7TF BROKEN "NUM"
1878 7TF TRIPLED EYE
1878 7TF QUADRUPLED STARS
1878 7TF DOUBLED DATE
1878 7TF TDO "R"
1878 7TF POLISHED "L"
1878 7TF SHORT LEAF
1878 7TF "N" CLASH
1878 7TF FACE CHIPS
1878 7TF WEAK "L"
1878 7TF WIDE REEDS
1878 7TF SLASHED "O"
1878 CC DDO LEAVES
1878 CC WING LINES
1878 CC DDO & LUMP
1878 S DDO "RIB"
1878 S LONG NOCK REVERSE
1878 S DENTICLE CLASH
1878 S TORN BONNET
1878 S TRIPLED EYELID

1878 S FUNKY FEATHER
1879 CC CAPPED CC
1879 O O/HORIZ O
1879 S REV OF 78
1880 KNOB 8 EDS
1880 KNOB 8 LDS
1880 8/7 SPIKES
1880 8/7 CROSSBAR
1880 8/7 EARS
1880 8/7 STEM
1880 8/7 CHECK MARK
1880/79
1880/9
1880/9 ATOP 0 CLASHED
1880 CC REV OF 78
1880 8/7 CC HIGH 7
1880 8/7 CC LOW 7
1880/79 O MICRO O
1880 8/7 O OVAL O
1880 8/7 O EAR
1880 8/7 O EAR & CLASH
1880 O DDO EAR
1880 O HANGNAIL
1880/79 S
1880/79 S LARGE S
1880 8/7 S CROSSBAR
1880 8/7 S MEDIUM S
1880/9 S MEDIUM S
1881 CC GOUGED "8"
1881 O PUMMLED EYE
1881 O GOUGED "O"
1881 O DDO EAR
1881 S WOUNDED EAGLE
1882 CC MISPLACED DATE
1882 CC COUNTER CLASH
1882 CC REVERSE DIE GOUGES
1882 O/S
1882 O/S FLUSH S
1882 O/S RECESSED
1882 O/S BROKEN
1882 O/O
1883 SEXTUPLED STARS
1883/1883
1883 O/O
1883 O "E" CLASH
1884 "E" CLASH
1884 LARGE DOT
1884 SMALL DOT
1884 DDO EAR

Error Coin Dates

Morgan Dollar

1884 18/18
1884 O/O
1884 O MPD "188"
1884 O DDO EYELID
1885 PITTED REVERSE
1885 CC DASH & ARROWS
1885 CC DOUBLED DASH
1885 S/S
1885 S/S MPD
1886 LINE IN "6"
1886 "3+2" CLASH
1886 DDR ARROWS
1886/1886
1886 GOUGE IN "M"
1886 O "E" CLASH
1886 O "BER" CLASH
1886 O "BER" & "T" CLASH
1886 O/O
1886 O "2+2" CLASH
1886 S/S
1887 "E" CLASH
1887/6
1887/1887
1887 DDO GATOR EYE
1887 DDO GATOR & CLASH
1887 DONKEY TAIL
1887/1—7 O
1887/6 O
1887 O DDO STARS
1887 O DDO PITTED REVERSE
1887 O "TY CLASH
1887 S/S
1887 S/S DAMAGED DENTICLES
1887/1—7 S
1887/1—7 S DOUBLED REVERSE
1888 DDR
1888 DDR & CLASH
1888 DDR DIE SCRATCH
1888 DDR DIE GOUGES
1888 DDR WREATH
1888 DDO EAR
1888 DDO EAR & CLASH
1888 DDO EYELID & MPD
1888 O "E" CLASH
1888 O DIE BREAK OBVERSE
1888 O DBO SCARFACE
1888 O DDO HOT LIPS
1888 O SHOOTING STAR
1888 O DDR ARROWS

1888 O/O
1888 O OVAL O
1888 S PITTED REVERSE
1888 S GOUGED EAGLE
1889 PITTED & CLASHED
1889 DDO EAR
1889 BAR WING
1889 "IN" CLASH
1889 O "E" CLASH
1889/18-9 O
1889 O WEAK "E" CLASH
1889 O OVAL O
1889 CC TAIL BAR
1889 O COMET
1889 O COMET & GOUGE
1890 O DDO EAR & LEAVES
1891 DDO EAR
1891 DDO EAR MOUSTACHE EDS
1891 DDO EAR & CLASH
1891 CC SPITTING EAGLE
1891 CC SPITTING EAGLE FAR DATE
1891 O "E" CLASH
1891 O "E" CLASH & EYE
1891 O "E" CLASH & GOUGE
1891 O PTITED REVERSE
1891 O WEAK "E" CLASH
1891 S DDO STARS
1892 O DDO EAR
1892/1892 S
1892 S TDO HAIR
1893 DDO STAR
1895 S/S
1895 S/HORIZ S
1896 DDO STARS
1896 DDO STARS & GOUGES
1896 MPD "8"
1896 BAR "6"
1896 O MICRO O
1896 O SHIFTED DATE
1896 S/S
1897 PITTED REVERSE
1897 DDO STARS
1899 O MICRO O
1899 O MICRO O GSA SOFT PACK
1889 O MIRCO O WING LINES
1899/99 S
1900 DDR ARROWS
1900 DDR & OLIVES
1900 MPD & DDR OLIVES

Error Coin Dates

Morgan Dollar

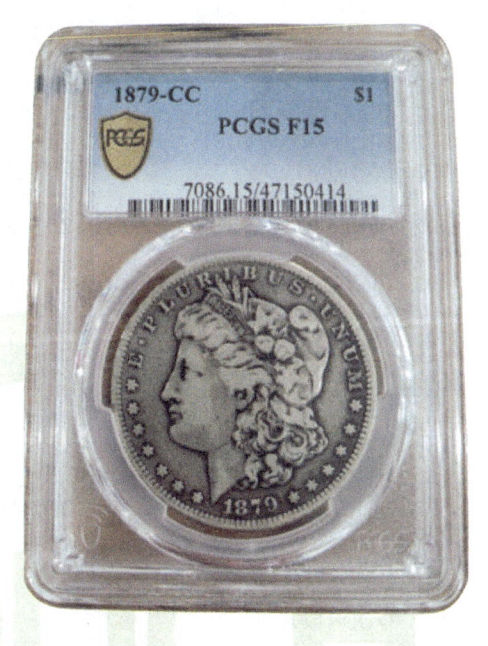

1900 O MIRCO O
1900 O DDO STARS
1900 O DDO STARS & CLASH
1900 O DIE BREAK DATE
1900 O/CC
1900 O/O/CC
1900/00 O/CC
1901 DDR FEATHERS
1901 DDR ARROWS
1901 DDO EAR & DDR OLIVE
1901 DDO EAR & EYE
1902 DDO EAR
1902 O MIRCO O
1902 O DDO EYE & EAR
1903 S SMALL S
1904 O FISH HOOK
1921 PITTED REVERSE
1921 PITTED & CLASHED
1921 WIDE REEDS
1921 DENTICLE CLASH
1921 D CAPPED "R"
1921 D CAPPED "R" FILLED "E"
1921 D UNICORN
1921 D UNICORN & CUD
1921 D DOUBLE CUD
1921 S THORN HEAD
1921 S GSA SOFT PACK
1921 S "B-U"
1921 S "B-U" & FILLED "S"

Error Coin Dates

Peace Dollar

1921 HIGH RELIEF
1921 RAY THROUGH "L"
1922 LINE IN TIARA
1922 FIELD BREAK EDS
1922 FIELD BREAK LDS
1922 EAR RING EDS
1922 EXTRA HAIR
1922 WINGBREAK & GOUGE
1922 HAIR PIN
1922 DDO MOTTO
1922 TDR LEAVES
1922 TDR & GOUGE
1922 SCAR CHEEK
1922 SCAR CHEEK & HAIR
1922 TDR & WING BREAK
1922 TDR & ERODED FACE
1922 DDR LEAVES
1922 DDR LEAVES & CRACK
1922 DDR WING
1922 DDO TIARA
1922 MOUSTACHE
1922 D DDR LEAVES
1922 D LEAVES & CRACK
1922 D DDO MOTTO
1922 D TDR LEAVES
1922 D TDR LEAVES & CLASH
1922 S TDR FEATHERS
1923 WHISKER JAW
1923 WHISKER & CRACK
1923 EXTRA HAIR
1923 TAIL ON "O"
1923 WHISKER CHEEK
1923 BROKEN WING
1923 CHIN BAR
1923 BAR WING
1923 DDO TIARA
1923 DDO TIARA & BREAK
1923 DDR LEAVES
1923 DDR LEAVES & BREAK
1923 D DDR EAGLE
1923 S PITTED REVERSE
1924 BAR "D"
1924 BAR "D" CRACK
1924 DDR EAGLE
1924 BROKEN WING
1924 EXTRA HAIR

1924 S DDR FEATHERS
1925 LINE IN TIARA
1925 MISSING RAY
1925 DDR SHOULDER
1925 S DDR LEAVES
1925 S DDR WING
1926 DDR LEAVES
1926 S DOT REVERSE
1926 DDR "DO"
1927 DDO
1927 D DDO
1927 S DDR LEAVES
1928 S DDO MOTTO
1928 S DDO MOTTO & LINES
1934 D SMALL D DDO MOTTO
1934 D LARGE D DDO MOTTO
1934 S DDO TIARA
1935 S 4 RAYS DDR LEAVES

Error Coin Dates

Eisenhower Dollar
1971 S DDO SILVER TYPE PROOF
1971 S DDO SILVER PROOF
1971 S TDO SILVER PROOF
1971 S SILVER "PEG LEG"
1971 S DDR SILVER PROOF
1971 D FRIENDLY EAGLE
1971 S SILVER "PEG LEG"
1971 S/S SILVER
1972 S DDO SILVER PROOF
1972 TYPE 1
1972 TYPE 2
1972 TYPE 3
1972 D DDR
1972 D DDO & DDR
1973 S DDR CLAD PROOF
1973 S DDO SILVER PROOF
1776-1976 S TYPE 1 CLAD PROOF
1776-1976 S TYPE 2 CLAD PROOF
1776-1976 TYPE 1
1776-1976 TYPE 2
1776-1976 D TYPE 1
1776-1976 D TYPE 2

Here is an example of a 1972 silver clad proof Eisenhower dollar coin.

Susan B. Anthony Dollar
1979 P NARROW RIM
1979 P WIDE RIM

Sacagawea Dollar
2000 P CHEERIOS PROMOTION
2000 P PROTOTYPE REVERSE
2000 P SPEARED EAGLE

Presidential Dollar
2007 P WASHINGTON ELONGATED RAY

PCGS
THE STANDARD FOR THE RARE COIN INDUSTRY
HAVE YOUR COINS GRADED & ENCAPSULATED BY THE MOST TRUSTED BRAND IN THE INDUSTRY
GET STARTED
PCGS.COM
MAXIMIZE VALUE, SECURITY AND LIQUIDITY
JOIN THE LARGEST COIN COMMUNITY & BENEFIT FROM OUR LIBRARY OF FREE NUMISMATIC APPS / RESOURCES
GET IT ON Google Play
Download on the App Store
PCGS.COM/APPS

Coin Grading

Coin grading is the process of authenticating and determining a coins condition. The coin grading scale is a 70 point scale created by William Herbert Sheldon. A "70" is the best grade a coin can receive. Typically the higher the grade, the more valuable the coin can be. It all depends on the population of the coin in a specific condition.

Secure Gold Shield →

Coin Holder

Date → 1995

Denomination → 1C

Coin Grade → PCGS MS66RD

Error → Doubled Die Obverse

Certification Number → 3127.66/37186785

Secure Gold Shield: This is a security element created by PCGS to make their labels impossible to replicate.

Certification Number: This reveals a coins population. The number represents the count of the number of coins in the same condition. Each number is linked to PCGS price guide and their Cert Verification app.

Coin Grading
Coin Grading Companies

Once you are certain you have a coin that should be graded, you can choose a coin grading company to have your coins condition determined and authenticated.

Here are four different coin grading companies. You can review each website and determine which is the best option for you. I personally have a PCGS membership. It is totally your choice who you chose.

Prices vary for each company and of course prices also vary for different types of coins. You will see that information on their websites.

www.PCGS.com

www.ngccoin.com

www.anacs.com

www.cacgrading.com

www.icgcoin.com

Coin Grading

Coin Grading Companies

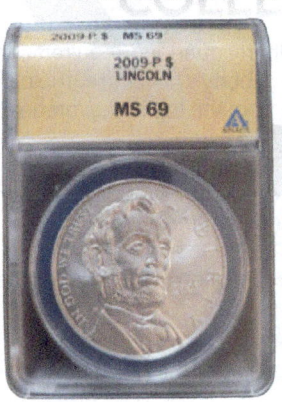

186

Coin Grading
Coin Grading Abbreviations

Here are some abbreviations you will want to be familiar with when reading your coin holders.

MS (Mint State): the grades for these coins are MS-60 to MS-70. Mint state is a business strike coin has never been in circulation.

PR (Proof): Proof coins are very detailed because they usually are given more than one blow from a die and are struck at a slower speed and higher striking pressures unlike business strike coins.

SP (Specimen): These are special coins struck at the mint from 1792-1816 that have similar characteristics as later proof coins.

RD (Red): This refers to copper coins that have more than 95% of their original red color.

RB (Red Brown): This refers to copper coins that have between 5% and 95% of their original red color.

BN (Brown): This refers to copper coins that have less than 5% of their original red color.

FS (Full Steps): This refers to the Jefferson nickel reverse. All 5 steps must be full with no damage or interruptions. FS also refers to first strike for specific coins.

FB (Full Bands): The bands on the reverse of the Mercury dime must be separated from left to right, without any damage, breaks, or gaps.

FH (Full Head): This refers to the Standing Liberty quarters. Requirements include, three leaves that must be clear and distinct in Liberty's hair, the earhole must also be present, and the hairline has to be distinct from the top of the forehead to the back of the neck.

FBL (Full Bell Lines): This is referring to the reverse of the Franklin half dollar coin. The bell lines on the bell must be complete and uninterrupted.

PL (Proof Like): These coins will have a clear reflection in the fields of the coin on both sides from 2-4 inches away.

DC (Deep Cameo): These proof coins will be heavily frosted on both sides of the coin.

SF (Satin Finish): These coins will have a smooth, lightly sandblasted look to them.

SMS (Special Mint Set): These are a special set of coins that are not business strike coins or proof coins. They were struck in 1965 and released the for the next couple of years. This was intentionally done by the mint to replace proof sets and to stop coin hoarding.

Silver Coins
Silver Coin Dates

Jefferson Nickel: 35% Silver (1942 -1945), they will have a large mint mark on the reverse of the of the coin above the Monticello.

Mercury Dime: 90% silver (1916 -1945)

Roosevelt Dime: 90% Silver (1946 -1964)

Washington Quarter: 90% Silver (1932 -1964)

Washington Quarter: 40% Silver (1776 -1976 S Bicentennial)

Walking Liberty Half Dollar: 90% Silver (1916 -1947)

Franklin Half Dollar: 90% Silver (1948 -1963)

Selling Coins

The number one most asked question on Couch Collectibles YouTube channel is how to sell your coins. Here are my 5 steps to selling coins. See the next page for the BEST place to sell your coins.

1. Gain knowledge through research about which coins you actually have. I hope my videos and this book have helped you to do that. Is it a high graded coin? or a low mintage key date coin? Perhaps you have silver coins or even a mint error coin. Learn about your coins first. I provide many videos on Couch Collectibles YouTube Channel about which coins to look for.

2. Once you know what you have, go to eBay, search for a coin similar to yours and click on sold listings. You will see what other coins have sold for in past auctions in similar conditions.

3. Be careful! If a coin is graded, it is typically going to sell for more than a raw or ungraded coin. if you find that similar coins have sold for hundreds of dollars, it may be a good idea to select a coin grading company to have your coin authenticated. The grade can affect a coins value tremendously.

4. If your certain you've found a rare coin and you know it's worth hundreds or even thousands of dollars and you proceed with having it graded, go back to sold listings on eBay and see what similar coins have sold for with the same grade. Then you will have a price range of what your coin could sell for after it has been graded.

5. Now it's time to sell your coin(s). You can sell your coins on Whatnot, eBay, Facebook Marketplace, Heritage Auctions, Craigslist, Offer Up, or even to a coin dealer or at a coin show. If you do not know how to sell on these platforms, watch a short video on YouTube about how to sell an item on Whatnot, eBay or Facebook.

Selling Coins

Sell Coins on the Whatnot App

The Whatnot app has totally changed the game when it comes to selling coins and collectibles.

I have a link on this page where you can sign up to become a Whanot seller. I personally sell coins on the Whatnot app 2-3 days per week and giveaway free silver coins or silver bars every auction!

Use the link below to become a seller on the Whatnot app. Please only use the link if you would like to be a long time seller.

Become a Whatnot Seller

https://www.whatnot.com/invite/seller/couchcollectibles

Coin Terminology
Glossary

Alloy: A mixture of two or more metals.

American Numismatic Association (ANA): they are a nonprofit educational organization that encourages numismatics.

Annealing: Heating blanks or "planchets" in a furnace resulting with the metal being softened.

Assay: To analyze and determine the purity of a metal.

Bag Mark: This is a mark on a coin from having contact with other coins in a mint bag.

Blank: This is basically a planchet. It is a blank piece of metal before the coin design is struck onto it.

Bullion: This is platinum, gold or silver bars and some coins.

Bullion Coin: These are precious metal coins sold for the current bullion prices.

Business Strike: This is a coin produced for circulation. You will find these coins in your every day pocket change unlike proof or uncirculated coins which are not made for circulation.

Bust: This is a portrait on a coin. For an example, it could be the head, neck and upper shoulders.

Clad Coinage: These coins have a core and outer layer made of different metals such as an inner copper layer on clad quarters, dimes, etc. Since 1965, all circulating U.S. dimes, quarters, half dollars, and dollars have been clad.

Collar: This is a metal piece that restrains the expanding metal of a planchet during striking process.

Commemorative: A coin or medal created to honor a person, place, or event. You'll see many of these for the Olympic silver coins.

Condition: The physical state of a coin.

Counterfeit: Of course these are fake coins or other pieces of currency made so that people will assume they are genuine.

Currency: Any kind of money that's used as a medium of exchange.

CRH: This abbreviation refers to Coin Roll Hunting, or the searching of desirable coins from banks.

Denomination: The different values of money.

Coin Terminology
Glossary

Die: An engraved stamp used for impressing a design on a blank piece of metal to create a coin.

Designer: The artist who creates a coin's design.

Edge: This is the outer border of a coin, or rather the side of the coin.

Engraver: An artist who sculpts a clay model of a coin's design.

Error: These are created when a coin is improperly produced. They can be overlooked in production and released into circulation.

Face Value: The amount a coin can be spent or exchanged for (a quarter's face value is 25¢).

Field: The part of the coin's surface that is not used for design or inscription.

Grade: Rating which indicates how much a coin has worn from circulation. The coin grading scale ranges from 1-70, with seventy being the best grade.

Hairlines: Tiny lines or scratches on coins, usually caused by cleaning or polishing.

Incuse: This is the part of a coin's design that is pressed into the surface.

Inscription: Words stamped on a coin or medal.

Intrinsic Value (Bullion Value): Current market value of the precious metal in a coin.

Key Date: These are low mintage coins or scarce dates that are usually more difficult to find.

Legal Tender: Coins, dollar bills or any other currency issued by a government as official money.

Legend: Principal lettering on a coin.

Medal: A metal object similar to a coin created to recognize an event, place, person or group. Medal's are not legal tender and are not intended to circulate as money.

Medium of Exchange: Anything that people agree has a certain value.

Mint: A location where coins of a country are manufactured under government authority.

Mint Luster: The dull, frosty, or satiny shine found on uncirculated coins.

Coin Terminology
Glossary

Mint Mark: A small letter on a coin identifying which of the United States Mint's facilities struck the coin.

Mint Set: A complete set of coins of each denomination produced by a particular mint.

Mint State: Same as uncirculated.

Mintage: The number of coins produced.

Motto: A word, sentence or phrase inscribed on a coin. For an example, "E Pluribus Unum" on U.S. coins is Latin for "out of many, one".

Numismatics: The study and collecting of things that are used as money, including coins, tokens, paper bills, and medals.

Obsolete: A coin design or type that is no longer produced.

Obverse: The front of a coin.

Off-Center: A coin that has received a misaligned strike from the coin press and has portions of its design missing.

Overstrike: A coin that is being produced with a previously struck coin used as the planchet.

Planchet: The blank piece of metal that a coin design is stamped onto.

Proof: A proof coin is made from highly polished planchets and dies are often struck more than once to give the coin great detail. These coins get the highest quality strike possible resulting in a mirror-like shiny appearance.

Proof Set: A set of proof coins of each denomination produced in a single year.

Relief: The part of a coin's design that is raised above the surface.

Restrike: A coin that is minted using the original dies but at a later date.

Reverse: The back of a coin.

Riddler: A machine that screens out blank planchets that are the wrong size or shape.

Rim: The raised edge on the sides of a coin.

Coin Terminology
Glossary

Roll: Coins that are packaged in coin rollers by people, banks, dealers, and the United States Mint.

Series: A collection of coins that include all date and mint marks of a specific design and denomination.

Slab: Nickname for a coin holder that coin grading companies use to encapsulate a coin.

Strike: The process of stamping a blank planchet with a coin's design.

Type Set: These sets are a collection of coins based on the denomination.

Uncirculated: This can refer to the manufacturing process by which a coin is created, or it could be used as a grade. It can even refer to a coin that has not been used in circulation.

Made in the USA
Monee, IL
03 February 2025